the
Origin
of the
Chinese
People

the Origin *of the* Chinese People

JOHN ROSS D.D.

Pelanduk Publications

www.pelanduk.com

Published by
Pelanduk Publications (M) Sdn. Bhd.
(Co. No: 113307-W)
12 Jalan SS13/3E, Subang Jaya Industrial Estate,
47500 Subang Jaya, Selangor Darul Ehsan,
Malaysia.

Address all correspondence to:
Pelanduk Publications (M) Sdn. Bhd.,
P.O. Box 8265, 46785 Kelana Jaya,
Selangor Darul Ehsan, Malaysia.

Check out our website at *www.pelanduk.com*
e-mail: *mypp@tm.net.my*

1st printing 1990
2nd printing 1994
3rd printing 2001

Perpustakaan Negara Malaysia   Cataloguing-in-Publication Data

Ross, John
    The origin of the Chinese people / John Ross.
    ISBN 967-978-336-7
    1. China – Civilization. 2. China – History.
    3. Chinese. I. Title
    909.04951

Printed by
Kit Sang Press Sdn. Bhd.

CONTENTS

iii

PREFACE

By H. A. GILES, LL.D., *Professor of Chinese Language and Literature at the University of Cambridge.*

THE death of Dr Ross was a distinct blow to the advancement of Chinese studies. His work, especially in connexion with Manchuria and Korea, needs no bush : had he lived, he would no doubt have added to this volume a prefatory note, which I have now been asked to supply.

In his researches into the origin of the Chinese people, Dr Ross would have nothing to do with the fantastic and unsubstantiated theory which traces the civilization of China, and particularly her script, to the ancient inhabitants of Accadia. His sober judgment claimed that the quest should be carried out among the voluminous records which China herself has to show ; and from such sources he derived many forcible arguments, which he has marshalled with considerable skill.

The period here covered begins with the semi-mythical age, some forty-six centuries before Christ, and ends with the Han dynasty, down to about one hundred years before the Christian era. Numerous illustrations of former Chinese rulers and sages, taken from early sculptures, lend an exceptional interest to the book, as also an exhaustive survey, with plates, of the development of the Chinese script.

Dr Ross declares (p. 50) that "we are justified in concluding that the Chinese people are autochthonous, and their civilization indigenous." In this important statement I entirely agree with him; but it must not be further assumed that I accept all Dr Ross' conclusions, or even admit the strict accuracy of every detail. A few points raised will be found, as specimens, on the following page; such discrepancies, however, do not seriously mar the general value of the book.

Notes by Professor Giles.

Page 26, last line, "Mother of Tsengtsu exhorting her son." This should *read*, "Mother of Mencius snapping the thread of the woof, and showing her son that work without continuity is of no avail."

Page 28, heading and elsewhere, for *Chin* read *Ch'in*. [Aspirates are insufficiently marked in other places ; the aspirate is specially important here, as there is another dynasty which is *Chin*.]

Page 30, line 8, and note. It has been satisfactorily established that "Si-wang-mu" was the Greek goddess Hera.

Page 36, Illustration. The meeting of Confucius and Lao Tzŭ has no historical basis.

Page 96, line 21. "Consistently—synonymous" cannot be substantiated.

Page 104, line 4. The symbol rendered "king" is not "king" at all, but quite a different symbol, though like in form. This vitiates the sense thus derived by analysis.

The Origin of the Chinese People

INTRODUCTION

THE Chinese are a people so unique in their character and in the prolongation of their existence that the investigation of their origin presents a study of singular fascination. Where is the site of their origin ? What are their affinities with and differences from other peoples ? Is their descent traceable to any other nationality ? How came they to form a separate nation ? They possess a remarkable form of civilization ; how came it to exist, and how was it developed ? Not a few writers have attempted the solution of these questions, but as the attempts have been mostly guess-work, the solution is yet to find. The isolation of the Chinese people has been so complete that their own literature is the only source where correct solutions can be found. Hence the present attempt to dig a little into that mine. No form of civilization has yet been found which has sprung, Minerva like, at one bound from the depths of savagery to perfect order. Such a change is conceivable only when one people borrows the civilization already existing among another people. The process of attaining to civilization from its lowest beginnings resembles the process universal in nature, from the bud to the ripening fruit. In the case of a people like the Chinese, so isolated and differentiated from others, this slow process is to be looked for.

Of the condition called civilization there may be endless varieties. Whatever raises a set of human beings above the life of the "birds and beasts" is a degree of civilization. From the savage life there are many degrees before we arrive at the highest form of Christian life. And these degrees may not inconceivably differ from each other. Manners, customs, government, literature, religion, are all involved in civilization. These forms may differ in different countries. Minds of a parochial type can perceive only one sort of civilization —that of their own parish. One such mind whose civilization consists mainly in military order calls another a barbarian becauses it refuses to be ridden by him ; the other calls the military type barbarian because he seeks to ride on him. Both are civilized, but the civilization of each is incomplete. The civilization of even the foremost nations of the west has not yet attained the ideal. It is not difficult to imagine a world, every man and woman in which shall be the equal of the best who has ever appeared, and possess talents as notable as the greatest of the past. It is conceivable that the world shall rise to a civilization as superior to the present as the present at its best is above the Middle Ages.

Though the Chinese are denied the possession of a civilization on the same plane as that of the west, yet their form of civilization, manifested in their social institutions, is worthy of serious attention. An acquaintance with that civilization is all the more desirable when we consider that China has entered on a new phase of life which cannot fail to exert a profound influence on the future of humanity. If her civilization differs little from that of her neighbours, it is because neighbours have imperfectly borrowed hers, who has borrowed from no one. This independence adds a further element of interest to the study.

The civilization of China is the outcome of a set of complex ideals, beginning with a lowly origin, stimulated, strengthened, and broadened during the course of many centuries by the efforts of a long succession of able men in many districts. These ideals embrace the method of government, the system of ethics, which conditioned their social life in all its relations, the theory of education, and the development of their script.

Now, the only satisfactory means of understanding the origin and development of this civilization is by the careful examination of Chinese Records. Theoretical comparison with the rise of civilization in the west is untrustworthy. To secure accuracy in this examination, one must bring a receptive and unbiassed mind, so as to discover the actual contents of the records, and to draw conclusions from them, instead of interjecting one's own opinions into them. One examining Chinese literature with preconceived theories bends to these theories with more or less violence the contents of the text. The translation becomes coloured by the views of the translator.

It has been contended that the Chinese people and script are traceable to Babylon, and their philosophy to India.

It need surprise no one that among peoples, the origin of whose script consisted of more or less accurate outlines of the object indicated, there should to a certain extent occur a small proportion of resemblances in the forms of their script. The same is true of approximations in monosyllabic names such as have been traced between Chinese, Hebrew, and Celtic. But the wholly monosyllabic character of the Chinese language differentiates it from all others, Turanian no less than Aryan. The language has enlarged its vocabulary to an enormous extent, but has retained unchanged its original character and grammatical construction. It is consistent with the other features of Chinese civilization that the traditional diagrams in straight lines by Fuhi may have been the beginning of Chinese writing. But the most ancient characters incontrovertibly known to literature are those on the first bronze vessels which were made by the Shang dynasty for sacrificial purposes forty-six centuries ago.

The reproductions at the end of this book of the ancient forms of Chinese script from the time of the eight diagrams of Fuhi, through the Shang, Chow, and Chin dynasties to the times of Han, may be possibly considered to occupy too much space. But apparent redundancy in presenting the evidence of the beginning and development of the Chinese script has been adopted as preferable to a possible inadequacy. Careful comparison will show that the script of the early Chow was a gradual evolution out of the pictorial Shang; that the later Chow was equally an evolution from the early Chow; that the Chin, though professedly a new system, is simply a continuation of the late Chow, and that the Han continued the Chin. From the beginning there was a slow growth, an evolution but no revolution. During those twenty odd centuries there was a regular though slow growth out of the old roots: there is no evidence at any point of Chinese history of an entirely new system of script. From first to last there is a close family likeness despite the lapse of time, the increase of words, and the minor changes thereby made necessary. The pictorial forms of Shang were largely adopted by the early Chow. They were gradually eliminated, and other forms introduced better adapted to more rapid writing. But even after the picture had completely disappeared, its outline could be frequently traced in the new form of the word.

It will be noticed that the script of Fuhi was in straight lines, that of Chow, Shang, and Chin in curved lines, and that of Han was a reversal to the straight line. Though the contour of a word and the number of lines may differ, the new form can be seen to have been evolved out of the ancient. From the earliest of the Shang to the present time there has been no breaking away from the spirit of the Chinese script, though from various causes changes have been introduced in the mode of writing. The writing and grammatical construction are alike throughout characterised by a family resemblance. These characteristics as well as the language itself are unique among the languages of mankind.

The Han script differs chiefly in abandoning, probably for ornamental reasons, the curved lines and in reverting to the straight lines of Fuhi. By skilful ingenuity, the characters are made to balance symmetrically on both sides of the perpendicular middle of the word. From the time of Han to the present this method has been followed in the making of seals of all sorts, from those of the emperor down. In the reproduction of the circle of characters round the mirror of Han, it will be noted how the late forms of the seal character approximates to the common square one.

The resemblance between Chinese dualism and Zoroastrianism is slight and superficial. Zoroastrian dualism is one of antagonistic forces. The dual powers of nature in Chinese philosophy, though radically different, are complementary and necessary to each other and to the existence of all living organisms. King Wen developed his yang and yin dualism in his native kingdom west of the Yellow River, in the south-east of what is now Shensi. This happened in the twelfth century B.C., several hundred years before Zoroaster was born. In the end of the twelfth century, the Chow crossed the Yellow River and introduced that dualism into China. This dualism and its antecedent monotheism are fully explained in the "Original Religion of China."

In addition to their special purpose, the chapters on the rise of the Chow and Chin dynasties are intended to show the process and causes of the change of dynasty in China.

Examination for a period of many years of Chinese ancient literature, and familiarity with the various theories on the origin of the Chinese and their civilization, preclude the belief on my part in the possibility of the derivation from any region west of the Yellow River of any portion of that civilization. Prior to the third century before the Christian era there is no evidence of any intercourse between China which was east of the Yellow River and any part of Central Asia. Early Chinese history shows how masses of the nomadic races to the north and immediate west were expelled westwards, who found their way in after centuries into eastern Europe. There is no evidence of any such migration from the west eastwards into China. By all available testimony we are driven to the conclusion that the Chinese people are autochthonous, their script and every form of their civilization indigenous.

The various sections of this work, though in no part exhausting the information available, provide material adequate to enable the careful reader to form his own decided opinion.

A brief account of him who was the principal agent in systematising and popularising the combination of the government and ethics of China will help both to comprehend the combination and to understand its influence on the preservation of the nation. It seems, indeed, to the writer to be all but axiomatic that lack of a clear understanding of that combination is the chief reason why the mind of the Chinese has been so long unknown in the west. A clear understanding will adequately explain not only the continued existence, but also the growing importance of the nation, despite occasional ebbings in the flowing tide. Though an account of the government and ethics is essential to the complete understanding of Chinese civilization, the space demanded for an adequate statement is such as to preclude its appearance in this volume, which is confined to the history of the origin of the people and of their education.

Face to face with the present condition of Europe, one essential difference between the ancient governments farther west and that of China must be mentioned here, for it is worthy of serious consideration. The nemesis attending the establishing as a standard the law of the wild forest is manifest in Europe. It produced its extreme logical effect in ancient

Babylon and Assyria. Those western powers trusted for authority and influence to martial prowess, and paid little attention to ethical principles. From its beginning China reversed this order. Her history reveals many practical relapses from her own ideal, but they invariably brought their own retribution. In the west the soldier was set above the teacher ; in China the scholar was placed above the man of war. Those nations which trusted the sword perished by the sword ages ago. China, whose greatest and most honoured men trusted chiefly to moral force, continues to exist and even to expand.

The Beings anciently worshipped, the modes of that worship, the sacrifices offered and the design of them, and of the religious services connected with them, are minutely described in the " Original Religion of China," published by Oliphant, Anderson, & Ferrier, Edinburgh. The reader is respectfully referred to that work for what is known or knowable of the religion of China. The remarks in the present work on the Religion of Confucius are necessary, for religion is an essential though unobtrusive element in his character. Without a knowledge of it one cannot understand him.

The Chinese works on which this book is founded are the SHU, or history compiled by Confucius ; the TUNG-CHIEN-KANG-MU, by Chu Futsu ; the YI-CHIH-LU ; the imperial TUNG-CHIEN-KANG-MU ; the LI-TAI, an epitome of history and geography, and the LI-TAI-TUNG-CHIEN-YI-LAN. The latter four are general histories published at different times and for various reasons by the Manchu Government, to the order of the Emperor by companies of competent scholars. The YUEN-CHIEN is a great encyclopædia forming a storehouse of information on all subjects from the earliest times. The dictionary SHWO-WEN gives the earliest, and that of KANG-HI the latest investigations on Chinese script, on the sources of which, however, the only satisfactory authorities are the PO-KU-TU, the SI-CHING-KU-CHIEN, and the KIN-SHI-SO. These three important works are described in the section on Education.

The pictures of human subjects throughout the work are copied from the Kin-shi-so, which has an abundant variety reproduced from the walls of temples, etc. They were workmanship on stone in the middle of the Han dynasty. This pictorial work was executed within the two first Christian centuries. We are not to assume that the facial representations are a true likeness of the persons nominally represented. Yet they are all interesting as indicative of the clothing and manners at the beginning of the Christian era in China.

IMPORTANT DATES

Fuhi, B.C. 2957; capital, Chun, near modern Kaifeng, in Honan.

Shen-nung, B.C. 2737; first capital, Chu-fu, south-west of Shantung; second, Chun.

Whang-ti, B.C. 2597; capital, Cholu, now Pao-an-chow, in south Chihli.

Shao Hao, capital, Chufu.

Chuen-hu, B.C. 2513; capitals, Ku-hien and Kao-yang, both in Honan.

Ku, father of Yao; capital, Hao, now Yen-shih-hien, in Honan.

Yao, B.C. 2356; capital, Ping-yang, of Shansi.

Shun, B.C. 2255; capital, Pu-fan, now Puchow, of Shansi.

Yu, B.C. 2205; capital, Pingyang, founded Hia dynasty, same capital, 2205-1767. During last reign of Hia, "Accomplished" Tang was ruler of the small state of Shang. He founded the dynasty of

Shang, B.C. 1766-1123.

B.C. 1184-1134, Wen reigned in the kingdom of Chow, west of Yellow River.

In 1135 king Wu succeeded king Wen, and in 1122 became ruler of China.

B.C. 1325, Tan Fu founded the kingdom of Chow.

Chow, B.C. 1122-249.

Chin State occupied kingdom west of river; Prince Cheng began to reign in 249.

Chin, B.C. 221, Prince Cheng became Whang-ti, or first emperor of China.

B.C. 206, Chin ceased to exist.

Han, B.C. 206 to A.D. 220.

From B.C. 2205 to B.C. 256 the title of the ruler of China was Wang, or king.

In B.C. 221 the style was changed to Whang-ti, which continued till the Manchus were dethroned.

xvii

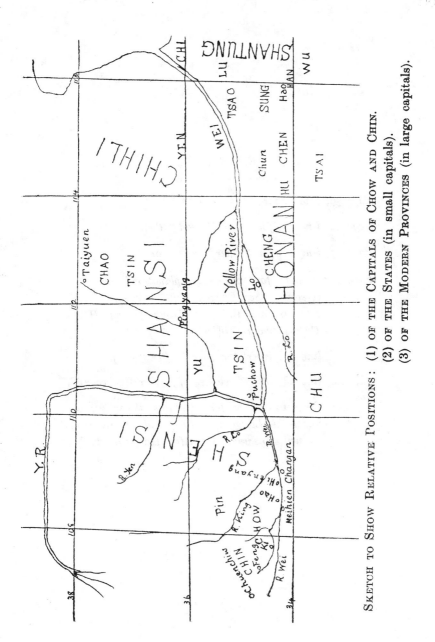

SKETCH TO SHOW RELATIVE POSITIONS: (1) OF THE CAPITALS OF CHOW AND CHIN.
(2) OF THE STATES (in small capitals).
(3) OF THE MODERN PROVINCES (in large capitals).

ERRATA.

Page 59, *line* 9. *for* " *Is* " *read* " *It.*"

Page 62, *line* 35, *for* " *thier* " *read* " *their.*"

Page 67, *line* 17, *for* " *other* " *read* " *one.*"

Page 115, *line* 15, *for* " *comment-explanation* " *read* " *inversion.*" *See Encycl. Britt.,* 11*th edn., vol.* VI, *p.* 219, *art. China,* § *Language, by* H. A. *Gi[les] and* L. *Gi[les].*

„   *line* 27, *insert* " *classes* " *after* " *simple.*"

„   *line* 28, *insert* " *classes of* " *after* " *compound.*"

Page 117, *lines* 19 *and* 20, *for* " *In the sixth century* A.D., *under the Liang dynasty* " *read* " *In the second century* A.D., *under the After-Han dynasty.*"

ORIGIN OF THE CHINESE PEOPLE.

SECTION I.—CHINESE PEOPLE AUTOCHTHONOUS.

CHAPTER I.

SEMI-MYTHICAL AGE.

THE design of the Book as compiled by Confucius was to delineate by historical references a form of government based on high moral principles. All traditions purely speculative were ignored. At the point where the History begins, China had already attained a high degree of civilisation. The beginnings of that civilisation are not mentioned nor the various stages in its progress. Other writers, both before and after him, who were less rigorously utilitarian, more curious, or more imaginative, ventured to peer into the darkness of the prehistoric ages. Though able critics of the Sung dynasty cautioned their readers against implicit faith in these traditional stories, some of them are too interesting to be left unnoticed.

A period of 2,267,000 years was computed to have intervened from the beginning of heaven and earth to the year 480 B.C. This period was divided into great sections, each with its own characteristics. Preceding that period were countless ages of one unbroken black night and the profoundest gloom. The universe consisted of Breath or Gas, which was a homogeneous unit without form. Out of this limitless chaos came the Great Limit, or Beginning. Then the grosser particles of the universal gas fell down and became Earth, the finer

A

ascended and became heaven. This was the beginning of
heaven and earth. These two in the course of many thousands
of years produced the four greater Bodies—sun, moon, planets
and constellations ; and the four lesser Bodies—water, fire,
earth, and stone. Then was the eternal stillness terminated.

Mrs FUHI.   FUHI.

(The serpent tail indicates wisdom.)

The interaction of these various bodies produced transformations, first of a simple then of a more complex kind, till they
finally culminated in the production of man.

Though man was the most intelligent of all beings, many
ages elapsed before the earliest rudiments of civilisation
appeared. Some of the remote ancestors of the Chinese dwelt

in caves, and wandered without fixed abode till one of their number devised a kind of dwelling, which put an end to cave homes. People of another tribe were naked, except for a small covering of plants before and another behind. One of them was a sage who cut wood into slices so thin that they could cover the body like fish scales and protect it from the winds and the frosts. He taught them to plait their hair so that the heaviest rain would drop off their head. Another tribe had no officials and no trouble. They lived together promiscuously like flocks of quails, and drank together like fledglings. Every one knew their mother ; no one knew his father. They could neither plead nor flatter. Their dead were suspended on trees till dried up by the wind.

The Nesting People were so called because they made for themselves nests for protection. Before their time, mankind lived among the beasts, with which they were on friendly relations. When men were clever enough to develop trickery, the inferior animals became their enemies. Against tooth, claw, horn, and poison, men were defenceless. Their sages taught them to combine pieces of wood to make a nest among the branches of trees and thus escape their foes. They could neither sow nor reap. They ate the kernels of nuts and the seeds of grass. They drank the blood of beasts and fowls, and ate the uncooked flesh of wild beasts with the hair on. With a piece of skin they covered themselves in front, and their back with another. In summer they found safety in the branches of trees, and dug deep pits wherein to shelter from the cold in winter.

The use of fire was discovered by the Fire People. From the bright stars above and the elements around them they inferred that there was in space such a thing as fire. When rubbing wood to polish it, they found that heat was evolved. When boring through wood, fire was actually produced. They learned how to use this fire for cooking food. Trees were divided by them into five varieties, according to their utility in making fire. They burnt elm and willow in spring, the date and apricot in summer, mulberry and pomegranate in mid-summer, oak and hornbeam in autumn, and in winter the locust tree and the beech. They were ignorant of letters, but recorded events by making knots on cords. Small knots were used to record minor, large for important events. They established markets for barter, and thus cultivated friendly relations.

In connection with these stories, the north of Honan is the only district mentioned. There, one listening to the notes of

神農氏因宜教田辟土種穀以振萬民

SHUNNUNG.

singing birds composed songs adapted to the voice of man to express the joyfulness of his heart.

The first historical name mentioned by Confucius is FUHI. He was said to have been miraculously born. In his time, thirty centuries B.C., the people lived promiscuously without marriage or family life. The only clothing known was the skins of animals killed for food. Fuhi instituted marriage and formal betrothal by means of a pre-nuptial present consisting of a deer skin, for then there was cloth neither of cotton nor of silk. He is credited with the first attempt at writing. From the various combinations of four long and four short lines, he formed the eight diagrams by means of which knotted cords fell into disuse. He also made the first attempts at chronology, by observation of the movements of the heavenly bodies. As appears in the chapter on Education, we cannot allow him the credit of instituting the Chinese script. His various institutions and improvements were the rude beginnings of a State. His capital was Chun, in the neighbourhhood of the modern Kaifeng, in Honan. Shunnung succeeded him in Chun, and removed subsequently to Chufu, in Shantung. He was so successful in growing the "five grains and hundred grasses" that he was elevated to the dignity of the god of Agriculture. He was followed by Whangti, who had become noted by his invention of wheels. The notion of rotary motion was suggested to him by the weeds he had seen whirled about by the winds. He constructed a chariot. His capital was in Kingshan, also in the neighbourhood of Kaifeng. He discovered copper, and commanded an official to cast twelve bells. He ordered another to make clothing, the outer garment black to represent the heavens, the inner yellow to represent the earth. Another was entrusted with the manufacture of earthen vessels. One of his wives was ordered to feed silkworms and to make silk cloth. Carts were constructed and boats built. A palace was erected, a portion of which was dedicated to the worship of Shangti, where sacrifice was offered. He divided the land into districts, and mapped out the territories occupied by the barbarians. He had many wives, and left twenty-five sons, of whom one succeeded him in Chufu. The following ruler was in Hao, now Kweite of Honan. The great Yao was in Pingyang of Shansi. By his time the various grades of officials were determined and social customs established.

From Fuhi to Yao a period of six centuries had elapsed. The names of the rulers are problematical, and the events recorded largely the product of a vivid imagination, though

they exhibit a slow process of improvement which is probable.
To us who are in search of the origin of the Chinese, the most
interesting portion of the ancient stories is the list of names of
the places given as the capitals of the earliest civilised life of
China. These are all confined to the bank of the Yellow
River, in the north-east of Honan and south-west of Shantung.

YAO.

Yao is the first name dissociated from that region. His
capital was in the south of Shansi, on the north bank of the
same river. All historical evidence points with unerring
finger to the neighbourhood of the Yellow River on its eastern

course along the northern border of Honan as the cradle of the Chinese people, and the place where originated its civilisation. All Chinese literature excludes the possibility of any connection between that origin and any land west of the Yellow River.

Not only was the original country of China confined to that narrow strip, it was surrounded on all sides by the rudest forms of barbarism. The beginnings of social change were of trifling extent. We are not shut up to infer that they were mostly the results of the energy of one man, or all evolved in one locality. Similar conditions of barbaric life existed over a vast extent of country. Where people were sparse and communication difficult, similar changes might co-exist in many places and arise independently and simultaneously. They depended on the appearing of a " sage," a man of unusual innate ability, able not only to devise but to influence others to adopt improvements.

The original moves in the civilisation of China were in the north-east of Honan. Geographically and socially, here was the Middle Kingdom. The surrounding inhabitants were barbarians, not because they were of a race differing from the Chinese, but because they refused to adopt the civilisation which was being evolved by a small community of their race. The various articles mentioned in the preceding pages—the grains, the trees, the fuel, the cotton and silk—were indigenous to that region. Farther south they could not all grow as the heat was too great and the cold was too severe farther north to mature them all. The Chow and the Chin dynasties are examples in historical times of peoples rising from barbarism to an equality of civilisation with the Chinese, and then raising the Chinese to a higher stage of civilisation than they had ever known.

The numbers quoted in the Mythical Age are unmistakably Chinese, but the terms describing the condition of the universe prior to the " opening of heaven and earth " bear a family resemblance to the first chapter of Genesis.

The terms explanatory of chaos can be traced to the commentators of the Sung dynasty. Now, in the seventh century, the Nestorian churches were widespread and their teaching influential over a great part of China, and especially prevalent in the capital, Sian-fu. After some centuries, their power had much diminished, and their number decreased. But they continued to exist, and became again influential under the Mongol dynasty. The Nestorians were familiar with the Chinese language, both literary and popular. It is but reasonable, therefore, to suppose that their teaching on the Creation was known to and pondered over by the scholars of Sung, who could adopt what would fill up the blank in their own classics on the subject of chaos.

CHAPTER II.

EMPEROR SHUN.

Shun, the second of the trio of rulers eulogised by Confucius, was born in the twenty-third century B.C. Yao, whose father had been chief of a small state south of the Yellow River, was then ruling over the tiny Middle Kingdom. His capital was in the south of Shansi, where Ping-yang now stands. Mencius states that Shun was an Eastern barbarian. His birthplace was in the depths of the mountains of Shantung. He lived surrounded by woods and rocks, and wandered among the deer and the swine. Shantung was then, with the exception of its south-west corner, entirely occupied by barbarians, of whom came Shun. His mother having died, his father married again. She bore a son, in whose interest the father desired to kill Shun. He fled westwards and made a settlement at Lishan, where he began farming and fishing. In his first year a crowd resorted to him. Next year the place became a township, and in the third year it was made the capital of a " kingdom " called Yu, which became a cognomen of Shun. It was located between the rivers Wei and Rui, in Hotung-hien of Hochung-fu. It was in Shantung. Shun differed in no respect from the wild men among whom he had lived. But when he heard a good word or saw a good deed, his joy resembled an overflowing river. Far removed from the influences of the civilised Middle Kingdom of the time, he received no instruction. But his personal character and his public life acquired for him a reputation which made him the successor of Yao and a model for all future rulers of China. This character he acquired by the faithful manner in which he uniformly conducted his life according to the innate disposition which Heaven confers on every man. In this he resembled Yao.

Sailing up the river from the land of Shun, along the west frontier of Shantung, we come upon Chufu and Chun, the cradle of the Chinese. Then sailing west on the north of Honan we come to the south-west corner of Shansi. Here we come to Ping-yang. On the west of the river is the land called Shensi. It was, from time immemorial, the dwelling-place of the ancestors of the Huns and Mongols. They did not cultivate the soil, but possessed herds of cattle and horses and flocks of sheep. Among these Western barbarians was born Wen, who was one of them. His birthplace was 1000 li from that of Shun, and his birth 1000 years after. He too was a man who diligently cultivated his inner disposition, so that his character resembled that of Shun so perfectly that they were like the " two halves of one seal."

Though the Mythical Age and the history of Shun prove the Chinese people to be autochthonous, yet on King Wen and his circumstances must be laid the heaviest end of the burden of proof.

CHAPTER III.

CHOW DYNASTY.

By the dynasty of Chow was consummated all that was great and good in China. Preceding dynasties initiated the rudimentary forms of civilisation, but laws, customs, ceremonial, ethics, and the first definite forms of the written character all trace their real beginning to Chow. The story of its rise and progress, is, therefore of more than ordinary interest. This story, as related by the historians of the later period of the dynasty is in its entirety incredible. Certain facts recorded are, however, not only credible but yield a probable account of the earliest beginnings of the civilisation which has guided China to the present. Examination of the historical dawn of Chow presents us, moreover, with valuable information as to the probable origin of the Chinese people. There exists both in the prose and poetical literature much that is mythical, more that is problematical, but not a little that bears the stamp of probability, and in this there is much to help us in our search.

The Chow historians assert that their people were the descendants of Howchi, founder of agriculture and minister of Yao. The narrative makes a great leap of six centuries from Howchi, and connects him with one Liw, who lived under the last king of the Hia dynasty. By this king, noted for his cruelty and vice, he suffered such persecution for some unknown reason that he fled from China, going westwards across the Yellow River to seek refuge among the nomadic inhabitants of Shensi. There, in B.C. 1796, he took up his abode at the foot of Mount Pin, where he commenced agricultural operations. These he conducted with such intelligence and industry, labouring day after day early and late, that he produced abundance of grain. With a wise liberality he secured the goodwill of his roving neighbours. His prosperity was so great that many of the natives abandoned their nomadic life and betook themselves to farming. They acquired herds of

KING WEN AND WIFE.

cattle and stores of grain, had enough for themselves and to spare for the wayfarer. His bounty was so freely given that his reputation spread widely, and men resorted to him from all quarters. His operations extended to the rivers Chi and Chu, affluents of the Wei, whose products he annexed. The people confided in his protection, relied on his faithfulness and sincerity, and praised his generosity. So many followed his example that he became head of a considerable community. Thus did he lay the foundation of the Chow kingdom.

After the lapse of four and a half unrecorded centuries, Tan Fu is said to have been head of Mount Pin settlement. His name appears in B.C. 1327 as descendant and successor of Liw. He was troubled by the nomadic barbarians who surrounded him on all sides. Mencius states that he lived among the Ti barbarians, who desired to "swallow him up." He offered them skins and cloth, which did not satisfy them. He presented horses and dogs, but they were not appeased. Pearls and jade did not purchase peace. Then he summoned the elderly men of his settlement, and said that what the Ti wanted was the cultivated land. There was a proverb to the effect that men should not injure others for the sake of those things intended for the use of man. There was no ruler in the land, therefore he suggested that he should leave that place and search out another situation for a new settlement. He then abandoned Pin and went south to Mount Ki, a distance of about eighty miles. The men of the Pin "kingdom" saying that he was a good man, followed him to the number of two thousand, like riders going to a fair.

In his new kingdom he speedily acquired so excellent a reputation that the people from neighbouring kingdoms adhered to him. To the new settlement he gave the name CHOW, signifying plenty. He was apparently satisfied with the change. The lessons of the past were not lost upon him. He introduced changes. He erected a fort, built houses, with rooms in which to live. The wall was surrounded by a moat. Within a year the houses inside that wall were completed, and in another year the fort became a " capital." He instituted five officials, one to oversee his followers, another to superintend the horses, a third to have charge of vacant ground, a fourth of cultivated lands, and the fifth to superin-

tend criminal affairs. His people praised him, and his reputation was widely extended. The exuberant poetical
rhetoric connected with these two founders of the Chow

SONS OF KING WEN.

dynasty may be read in the " Original Religion of China,"
pages 100-102.

To Tan Fu were born three sons. The youngest was Chili,

who had a son Chang, or Illuminator. This child exhibited promise of capacity so great that his grandfather prognosticated for him the possibility of raising Chow to be a great State. So unmistakable was the desire of the grandfather for Chang to be his successor, that the two older sons agreed to renounce their rights. They adopted the name of one of the nomadic tribes south of them. On the death of their father they retired to that tribe, assumed their dress and manners, and became subjects of their chief.

Chili succeeded to a kingdom considerably enlarged. This was probably due to the security of a walled town, and the permanency of dwelling-houses, by which the number and cohesion of his people were naturally increased. He was more aggressive than his predecessors. He and his people were necessarily more attached to the land on which their houses were built and the soil which they cultivated than were the nomads to the soil on which their tents were pitched for a brief season. He even marched beyond the land from which his father had been driven away, and defeated the Yung west of the river Lo. The king of Shang granted him the title of Mushi, or "Pastor." After he had defeated three other Yung kingdoms, he was made Si Po, or "Count of the West." The insignia of this office bestowed upon him were a stone sceptre, a cup, and fragrant herbs to mingle with strong drink when offering sacrifice. A few years thereafter he died, leaving a much enlarged kingdom to his son Chang.

TOPOGRAPHICAL.

At this stage it is advisable to explain clearly the topography of the cradle of the Chow dynasty. The Yellow River has for unknown ages divided the lands of Shansi and Shensi. It is laden with the detritus worn by atmospheric action from the sides of thousands of mountains, and carried by countless streams into the great river. The river in flood spread over immense areas of country, depositing its mud in all the hollows and forming plains of level lands of the richest soil. In the twenty-fourth century B.C. Yao made his capital in the south-west of Shansi, on the east bank of the river. There he and the small kingdom of which he was head cultivated the soil in a rude fashion. Ping-yang and its neighbourhood continued to be the most civilised portion of eastern Asia for almost six centuries. Across the river, directly west from the kingdom of Yao, was a boundless extent of country, chiefly mountainous, inhabited by nomads. They were big-boned, hardy, and fierce men, who disdained to defile their hands with labour in the soil. They dwelt in tents, possessed herds of cattle, flocks of sheep, and were rich in horses. They were of the Turanian race and speech. Their kingdoms were tribes, larger or smaller according to the wisdom or the prowess of the chief. Each puny kingdom had its own title, which was changed with a change in the ruling family. In the time of Yao the most powerful family in his neighbourhood was called the San Miao, which for a few centuries challenged the Middle Kingdom for supremacy. Other names occur at various periods, but all indicate the fierceness of their character. In the early Chow period the names were Yung (brutal) and Ti (violent), both names indicating the same fierce and lawless disposition. Other names occur in the story of Wu Wang. Each community under its own chief possessed its own grazing ground, which was jealously defended against encroachment by others. They were occasionally combined by the energy and skill of a great leader into a formidable army, such as that of the Huns, Turks, and Mongols. Each of these in turn fought with China before the Chinese began to traverse the far west.

LIW THE REFUGEE.

It was among the Yung west of the river that Liw sought a hiding-place from the wrath of the last king of Hia, who reigned east of the river. The capital of this king was not far removed from the river, and the place selected by Liw was near to the western bank. There, in the midst of a nomadic population, he began the life of strenuous devotion to agriculture in which his prosperity was so notable that his reputation became wide spread. A large community adhered to him, following the same occupation, and of such numbers as made it impossible that he could remain hidden. The success of this community in changing a wide extent of uncultivated land into numerous fruitful farms could not fail to be reported in Ping-yang. Had he desired to secure secrecy he would have been safer in some remote part of the agricultural lands of China than in the midst of a boundless country of nomads. Further, had he sought a hiding-place he would not have selected a point near his native land, where hiding was impossible. Had he fled farther west and adopted the manner of life in the country, his hiding-place would be safe against the least sign of recognition. If the man Liw therefore ever existed, it is impossible to accept the story that he was a fugitive from China, who, to avoid his king, took up his abode in the nomad country at no great distance across the river. That some one among the nomads adopted the life of the farmer from his observation of the Chinese life on the east side of the river is probable and reasonable, but that he was a refugee Chinaman is improbable. The large community of farmers forming the " kingdom " of Pin were nomads converted into farmers, and it is reasonable to infer that the first to adopt the agricultural life was himself one of the aboriginal nomads of the region.

The interval of four and a half centuries between Liw and Tan Fu is too great a blank to permit us to accept without question the family connection claimed between the two. The story of Tan Fu approaches near enough to the historical time of Wen Wang to enable us to accept it as probable. He established at the foot of Mount Ki a small compact kingdom of nomadic barbarians transformed by agriculture to civilised life. Exposure to plundering irruptions by their uncivilised neighbours compelled him to devote considerable attention to the art of war and of defence. He left an enlarged territory and extended influence to his son, who increased the territory and attained a military efficiency which defied attack. To this kingdom Chang the Illuminator became heir.

In the story there is no hint of the introduction of any Chinese individual or influence, though the nearness of more experienced agriculturists must have made its mark to a certain extent. Indeed, the governing power of China had by that time fallen to so low an ebb that it had little which it could teach any one. The Chinese possessed a written language, but of so limited an extent that the young state of Chow could afford to ignore it. Nor did the conditions of that state make literature, or even writing, a pressing need. Chow was ab-

B

solutely without letters, and we must remember that Mencius declared Chang to have been a western barbarian as Shun had been a member of the east barbarians.   He, his people and his lands, were all of the nomadic race, who had been transformed into a civilised people by the cultivation of the soil and the possession of a permanent home and location.

DUKE CHOW

The diligence, the wisdom, the justice, and the benevolence of Tan Fu congregated and welded together a large community of the Yung and the Ti barbarians, and laid the foundations of the Chow dynasty   A fortunate succession of similarly

minded men converted the neighbourhood of Mount Ki into
an independent and strong state. This was all the more easy
as the ruler of China was king in name only. It was in King
Wen, however, that all the good qualities of the founders of
Chow combined to make a character of such elevation that he
to this day is regarded as the real founder of the civilisation
of the Chinese nation.

WEN WANG.

Four and a half centuries before Tan Fu, the execrable
character of the last of the kings of Hia, the descendants of
Yu, combined with the brutality of his government, roused
universal hatred against him. South of the river, in Honan,
was a small state called Shang, whose ruler was famed for the
excellency of his private life and the wisdom of his government.
He was hailed as the avenger of the people of the empire, and
established the dynasty called Shang. This long-lived dynasty
moved its capital repeatedly in the north of Honan and the
south of Shansi. It occupied as its kingdom a narrow strip of
land on both sides of the Yellow River. The south of Shansi
and of Chihli, the south-west of Shantung, and the north of
Honan, embraced the entire extent of China in those days.
The dynasty decayed in wisdom and consequently in power
as the centuries glided by. On the occupation of a city called
Yin as capital, the dynasty assumed the title Yin. From this
capital its barbarian neighbours of the east, aggressive in
proportion to the weakness of China, drove it northwards
across the Yellow River, where a new capital was made at
Feiwei of Chihli. There the Yin dynasty was reigning when
Chang succeeded his father as Chief of Chow in the remote
west. His father, because of his military prowess against the
barbarians in the west, had been ennobled by the Yin dynasty
as count of the West. The title was hereditary, and Chang
became Si Po, or Count of the West, when he succeeded his
father. He continued to live in Ki as capital, and devoted
himself entirely to the welfare of the State. He formulated
laws; he instituted tithing of the produce of the land as
income for the government; he made office hereditary. To
meet the necessities of aged men and widows, the solitary who
were without means of support, and young orphans, all of

whom were the most helpless of the community, he enacted ordinances of benevolence. He commanded his followers to bury carefully the bones of dead men found in the wilds. The report of this incident spread over the whole empire, producing a most favourable impression, for if he so cared for the bones of the dead, how much more would he consider the needs of the living. He was polite to men of the lowest ranks if they were known to be men of good character. During daytime he ate sparingly that he might be able to attend at all times to any business. Ultimately the officials of Shang resorted to him when their advice was rejected by their own king. His

KING CHENG.

position was so strong that the king commanded him to oppose the Kunyi barbarians to the west, and the Hienyun to north of him. These names were prefixed by the word for " dog," because of the ferocious and intractable nature of their disposition. Their descendants were known as the Chuen Yung, and the Híwngnu—" dog " Yung and Huns.

The experiences of his ancestors compelled him to recognise the possibility of encroachment by his nomadic neighbours. To prevent calamitous wars in his own territories, he took all necessary precautions, by the closer cohesion and consolidation of his people. By their laborious diligence in cultivating their fields, they had gained an energetic and powerful physique.

Military training soon made them an effective check on the roving hordes. Ere long he made an expedition to Pin, whence his grandfather had been driven away, and took possession of it.

The last king of Yin was Chow Sin. In his first year he became notorious for extravagance and excessive drinking. He was the first to use ivory chop sticks. Censuring this extravagance, Kitsu, one of his ministers, said that " to-day it was ivory chop sticks, to-morrow it will be jade cups. The eating of bears' paws will follow. Such extravagance and covetousness will bring the empire to ruin." This incident reveals the economic condition of that time. The viciousness of Chow Sin developed rapidly, till, in his eleventh year, he was reported guilty of the wildest excesses, and the most brutal of murders. He had discarded every good and noble quality. Over the reports of such unnatural cruelty, the Count sighed in secret. His sentiments were known to his neighbouring chief, the Lord of Tsung, who accused him to the king of harbouring rebellious designs. He was seized and imprisoned for two years.

During his imprisonment he studied the eight diagrams of Fuhi, and extended them to sixty-four. In course of his studies he produced the Yi Ching, or Book of Transformations. By it he introduced the Dual System into China, which had till that time been monotheistic. He had ample opportunity for making the acquaintance of the few written characters evolved in China. The method of his deliverance is interesting.

His ministers were grieving over his imprisonment. One of them adopted a method accordant with the character of the King. From a tribe of the Yung he procured a young woman of uncommon beauty, piebald horses, a quartette of sets of chariot horses of a rare variety, each set consisting of four. These, with various other curiosities, he presented to the King to purchase the liberty of his lord. The King received the gifts joyfully, and set the prisoner free. The Count in his gratitude offered to the King the lands west of the river Lo, which was the first part of Shensi annexed to China. The King was so pleased that he granted to the Count a bow, arrows, a headman's and a battle axe, emblems implying the right of making war. He also granted the prayer of the Count for the abolition of branding. The Count's political creed is said to have involved the criminality of rebellion of what wickedness soever the King may have been guilty. This creed was not modified by his imprisonment. He restored to the King some " kingdoms " which had revolted.

In the year after his liberation, two Chiefs who could not agree as to their boundaries appealed to the Count. The two were named Yu and Rui, names of places now known as Pingliw and Ruicheng-hien of. Yungping-fu. When they crossed the frontier of Chow they noticed the farmers yielding to each other on points affecting their property. Travellers going in opposite directions obligingly yielded the right of way. Entering the city, they saw men and women walking each in their own street without jostling or pushing. Inside the Court, lower officials made way for the higher, and the higher for ministers. The Chiefs were charmed with the order everywhere prevailing, and confessed themselves unworthy to enter the palace of the noble man. They agreed to yield to each other, and made the land which had been subject of dispute neutral ground. They finished the business by acknowledging the Count as their feudal superior. The story was widely repeated, and forty " kingdoms " followed their example and submitted to the Count.

In his fifteenth year he attacked the " dog " Yung to his west, and annexed three other barbarian kingdoms to his domain in the three following years. In his nineteenth year he attacked the Chief of Tsung, who had calumniated him to the King, and took his territory. Here he erected a new capital, which he called Feng, situated to the west of the Feng river. In the new capital he built an observatory, which was called the Wonderful. It was erected for taking observations of the sun, moon, stars, and any celestial phenomena. Next year he died.

Though history magnifies his wars and annexations, mentioning the number of kingdoms which he amalgamated, yet Mencius declares that the extent of his kingdom was barely a hundred li square. It was wholly west of the Yellow River. His possessions were confined to the lands of the Yung and the Ti, who formed the population of his kingdom. That kingdom at its best was but a corner in the south-east of Shensi.

After he had established a reputation for wise and just

rule, prominent men who had abandoned the corrupt Chinese Court acceded to him. Mencius mentions two principal officials who left the wicked Chow Sin in disgust. One found a retreat on the shore of the north sea, the other on the shore of the east sea. They had heard the great name of the Count, and the manner in which he treated old men, and betook themselves to his Court. They possessed all the learning then known to China, and in time became the most notable men in the land. The accession of such men added lustre to his Court, and by increasing his knowledge made his influence still greater. From them he completed his knowledge of all the written characters of the Chinese, and the principles on which they were constructed. His land, his resources, his laws and ordinances, the friends who had been attracted by his character, the army, which he had thoroughly trained, formed the entire power with which his son went to wrestle for the throne of China.

The Count of the west, afterwards known as King Wen (literary), was buried at Pin, and at his tomb was performed the newly fixed Chow Ceremonial. He was succeeded in the kingdom and title of West Count by Fa, his oldest living son, who was even then an old man. He had married a daughter of Lu Shang, one of the prominent Chinese scholars who had joined his father. She bore one son. This Count was known as Wu Wang, or the Martial King.

Four years after his accession, this Wu Wang, when offering sacrifice on Mount Pin, saw in the distant east soldiers exercising at Mengchin, the Ford of Meng. A fish leaped on board his boat when in mid-stream crossing the river. On shore a fire descended from heaven into his room, where it changed to a flesh-coloured bird. The special significance of these omens we are unable to fathom. Of more importance was the revolt to him of eight hundred feudal princes, who had till then remained faithful to Chow Sin. They assembled at Mengchin, and unanimously declared that on account of his unparalleled wickedness, Chow Sin should be deposed. To this opinion the Count replied that without clear indication of the will of Heaven one could not say whether war should be declared.

The kingdom of Li (Licheng-hien of Lu-an-fu), east of the river, was attacked and seized by Wu, because of aggressive

GENERAL CHI.

trouble. The officer in charge fled to Chow Sin in terror to report. The king replied that his fate was at the disposal of Heaven, and refused to listen to any advice. He had degraded the minister Weitsu for admonishing him. For expostulation, Kitsu was imprisoned. Pikan, his uncle, blamed him for sentencing a minister to slavery and was put to death. The wicked folly of his Court was beyond imagination. Weitsu fled to Wu, taking with him the sacrificial vessels belonging to royalty. His cry that Chow Sin should be no longer tolerated brought matters to a crisis, and Wu decided for war.

He summoned to a Council of War all his men and the princes who adhered to him. He offered sacrifice to inform Heaven and Queen Earth* of his resolution. He sacrificed to the Spirits of the great mountains and notable rivers as he passed (for full description see " Original Religion of China"). In the first moon of the thirteenth year of his reign, he made his headquarters at Mengchin. There he administered the oath to the princes, the high ministers, the officials, the heads of soldiers, and the chiefs of the Yi and Ti who accompanied him from the west. By this oath he secured order and union in the heterogeneous mass. Next moon he drew up his army on the plain of Muye. It totalled 60,000 men. The Yung tribes contributed 300 chariots, and the princes 700. Eight nomadic kingdoms were represented under their chiefs. They were Yung, Shu, Chiang, Nei, Mao, Lung, Feng, and Pu. These were kingdoms located west and south-west of Chow, embracing eastern Thibet, and were of the racial divisions of Yung, Man, Ti, and Chiang. Chow Sin marched against him with a great army, which, because of the character of the king, did not wish his success. Many fled from the field, not a few joined the enemy, and those who remained refused to fight. Chow Sin, finding himself betrayed, fled and clothed himself in splendid array. In garments glittering with shining jewels and pearls, he mounted a tower and burnt himself to ashes.

The year was proclaimed the first of King Wu and of the Chow dynasty. It was B.C. 1122. Feng was abandoned as capital. A new one was established eight miles east of Feng, called Hao. Next month he made his numerous brothers feudal princes of the various states of his new kingdom. The

---

* The dual form Heaven and Earth is here introduced for the first time.

officials who had revolted to him retained their former offices. The nomadic chiefs were made high officials of China. He introduced many innovations, but had much spade work to do in the way of civilising his new subjects. In the following summer, all officials of the late dynasty presented themselves to acknowledge the new sovereign, and were reinstated in their former position.

MOTHER OF TSENGTSU EXHORTING HER SON.

The above are the more important facts connected with the origin and establishment of the Chow dynasty. Special attention is drawn to the fact that the most reliable part of the army of Wu was formed of the barbarians inhabiting the regions west and south-west of his own kingdom of Chow It was by this army the Chow dynasty was put and was kept on the throne of China. Their chiefs were made high officials of China. The men were enrolled in the ranks of the Chinese. In a couple of generations they were not only amalgamated with, but became indistinguishable from, the Chinese. The inferences deducible from the history of the rise of the Chow dynasty are exemplified in that of the Chin, which succeeded the Chow, and which, under its patronage, rose from nothing to greatness, as will appear in the following narrative.

CHAPTER IV.

CHIN DYNASTY.

After the Chow dynasty had introduced order into their new kingdom, enlarged its borders, increased its population by the assimilation of their nomadic followers and themselves, they unified the language, improved it, established schools to teach it, and got it into general use. They raised China to a position of power, influence, and education, to which it had never attained before. Having mounted to their zenith, they, after a few centuries, began to decline. They were ultimately supplanted by the Chin dynasty, the story of whose rise has an important bearing on our subject, as it illustrates the various steps in the progress from barbarism to civilisation, and also the manner in which one dynasty succeeded another in China. The story of the beginnings of this dynasty may not be generally interesting, yet an outline is necessary in order to understand its relation to the original people of China. This outline shall be as brief as is compatible with intelligibility.

As the dynasty of Chow traced their ancestry back to a famous personage of remote ages, the Chin could not be satisfied with an ancestry less illustrious. They claim descent from Chwan Su, grandson of Whang ti (2597). Nu Siw, granddaughter of Chwan Su, was weaving one day, when a blackbird dropped an egg, which she picked up and ate, with the result that she bore a son, who was called Daye. To him was born a son Dafei, who assisted Yu in clearing away the waters of the great flood. On the completion of the work, the Emperor conferred on Yu a black jade sceptre. When accepting it, he said that Dafei had been an excellent second, without whose aid he could not have finished the job. The sovereign then gifted Dafei with a black sceptre, second only to that of Yu, and said that his descendants would also attain to great fame. Dafei had two sons, one called Da-lien-shi-niao-su-shih, the other was Yomushifushih. Their descendants lived partly among the Chinese, partly among the Yi and Ti barbarians.

One section was devoted to the Shang dynasty. Feilien was attached to Chow Sin. He had a son of prodigious strength,

KING CHIN

who was killed when Chow Sin perished. He had another son thereafter, Meng Tseng, who secured the favour of King

Cheng (1115-1079). His grandson, Tsao Fu, was passionately fond of horses and of driving. King Mu made him charioteer. The chariot was drawn by four famous horses named after their colour.

In 985 the King drove westwards in his chariot, 2960 li from his capital, to the mountain Kunlun, near Sochow. When he arrived at the mountain he saw the mother of the west King, Si-wang-mu,* in her queenly state. In the mountain was a stone chamber. What with its pearls rounded and irregular, the carvings on the tower, the marvellous ornamentation, the place seemed the abode of deity. This was the Hall of the Mother. He was so overwhelmed at the sight that he forgot the business for which he got there, and returned. The author who gives that story relates a more reasonable cause for the King's return. The prince of Hu, a province on the extreme east of the kingdom, taking advantage of his lord's absence, rebelled against him. Tsao Fu, eager to see his master home to quell the rebellion, drove him back at the rate of 1000 li per day. As a reward the city of Chàocheng, east of the river, was gifted to him. He and his family were afterwards known as the Chao clan. The fifth generation from him was FEITSU, with whose name historians usually begin the story of Chin.

Apart from the genealogy of Chin, there is no historical foundation for most of the preceding statements. The name Chwan Su emerges in literature later than the time of Confucius. In the story of Yu there is no mention of such an one as Dafei ; the names of his two sons are certainly not Chinese. One is of six syllables, the other of five. They may have been handed down by tradition, as names connected with the beginnings of Chin. The Chao and Chin families are stated to have known the name of their mother, but not the name of their father. The statement coincides with what the Mythical Age calls the life of the " birds and beasts." The Chao lived among the nomads of northern Shansi, the Chin among those west of the river. The Chao became a powerful family, and were formidable rivals to the Chin. Neither was acquainted with the style of writing of the rude and simple kind used in the Middle

---

* This story is of more recent date than the Chin Dynasty. Compare Richard's " Mission to Heaven," p. 64.

Kingdom. What we are most interested to know is that the two were of nomadic, not of Chinese ancestry.

The point at which we have arrived demands more credence and claims more attention. Feitsu lived in Chwenchiw. He delighted in tending horses and cattle, which fattened rapidly under his care. King Hiao (909) heard of him, and commanded him to feed the royal horses in the district between Chien and Wei rivers. He was so gratified with the condition of the horses that he made their herdsman Superintendent of Horse, reviving in his person an old family name Ying, and

ARCHERS.

gifted him an estate CHIN (a kind of rice). Thus did the king of Chow lay the foundation of the Chin family in B.C. 897. It was laid, not on the basis of agriculture, but on that of cattle raising. It was in the territory of the original Chow.

Sixteen years after that date, the king of Chow, Li, was so oppressive a ruler, that the princes rebelled against him. The

West Yung destroyed his palace, slew the family of Feitsu, and took possession of Chwenchiw. When King Huen ascended the throne (827), he created Chin Chung, grandson of Feitsu, an official of China, entrusting him with the duty of punishing the Yung. He, being the first of his race to be elevated to office, set up chariots and horses, and adopted some of the ceremonial and music of China. He was slain by the Yung before he had collected forces adequate for attack. He had five sons, the oldest of whom succeeded him as " duke " Chwang. To him and his brothers the King gave a joint commission with 7000 men to attack the Yung. They were successful, and recovered Chwenchiw. He was elevated to be high official of Sichui. The second of his three sons succeeded him as Duke Siang. He removed his capital to Chienchang (near Lungchow).

In the second year of this duke, King Yow of Chow (781-771) disinherited his heir in favour of the son of his favourite concubine, Paoszu. The feudal princes rebelled, and, with the aid of the Yung and Chuen Yung, slew the King. Duke Siang marched to aid his King, and fought valiantly but unsuccessfully. He escorted the new King, Ping (770), to a new capital in the east of the kingdom, which had been divined to be a lucky place for a refuge against the formidable Yung of the west. Then did China become the Middle Kingdom, by retreating to the neighbourhood of the seat of the ancient dynasties. For his services the duke was created a feudal prince, and awarded the right to take possession of Feng and Ki, the original kingdom of Chow, which had been seized by the wild Yung.

Up to this time, the Chin could not use the ceremonial of the Chinese in their marriage forms. His rank as prince entitled Siang to the full Chinese ceremonial. He could also drive a chariot drawn by red horses with black manes. He erected a West Terrace as altar whereon to offer sacrifice to Shangti. He sacrificed three oxen and three he-goats. This proclaimed his rank to the world. He erected a palace called Sichi-hien after the altar. In the twelfth year of his reign he fought against the Yung, drove them out of Ki, occupied it, and died.

His son, Duke Wen, erected a palace in Sichi-hien. He

marched east to the junction of the Chien and the Wei with 700 men, on a hunting expedition. Divination proved this place, which had been gifted to his forefathers, as most appropriate for a capital. He built a fortified town there, which he called Meihien, by which name it continues to be known. He erected two altars in different places. He set up three prisons, there having been none before. He also appointed a Writer, whose duty it was to take note of national affairs. From this event dates the beginning of a gradually increasing civilisation. After he had cleared the Yung out of all the old lands of Chow, he promulgated a set of laws defining the crimes against the three relationships (parents, brothers, and one's family, or father, mother, and wife). He died in the fiftieth year of his reign, was buried in Sishan of Sihien. He was succeeded by his grandson duke Ning (715), who removed his capital to Pingyang, west of Kichow, annexed two small kingdoms to the westward and died. He was buried in Sishan, which came to be known as the Chin Tombs.

He left three sons, the oldest of whom was set aside and the second enthroned, but speedily murdered, when the oldest was recalled. He was known as Duke Wu (698). One of his first acts was the execution of his brother's murderer. He built a palace in Pingyang, and instituted the office of Cheng-siang, or Councillor. He converted two of the Yung settlements into the two first Hien cities, calling them Kwei and Ki. Two others he established in the east of his kingdom. He died and was buried in Pingyang. For him first were men slain to accompany him into the spirit world. Sixty-six were killed and buried with him. Duke Te, his successor (677), made his capital in Yung cheng, where he built a great palace. On one of the altars he sacrificed three hundred bullocks. From that time his kingdom extended rapidly. He instituted the periods called " Fu " in the great heat. In the Fu periods sickness was prevalent and death frequent. The evils were believed to be the work of bad spirits, whose nature was of the Yin principle. To counteract the mischief dogs were sacrificed. Their spirits are of the Yang principle, which, when thus liberated would destroy the other. After this institution, he died, leaving three sons, the oldest of whom succeeded as Duke Huen.

C

WAR AT A BRIDGE.

He erected an altar near the river Wei, making the fifth altar in the kingdom, each to a separate deity. He died after a reign of twelve years, most of which was spent in warring against the State of Tsin, his nearest neighbour east of the river. One of his nine sons succeeded him, followed by another in 660 as Duke Mu.

The Chow sovereign had long ceased to be real ruler, and the States were in a condition of perpetual internecine war. The princes of many States were murdered by men who seized the throne. Chin, being outside of China, was beyond the reach of the danger zone, and benefited accordingly.

In 658 the State of Tsin was afflicted with a grievous famine. The ruler appealed to Chin for help. His ministers recommended the duke to take advantage of the weakness of their enemy to destroy him. One minister protested against such a policy, for though the ruler of Tsin was their foe, that was no reason why the innocent people should suffer the calamity of starvation. The duke adopted this advice, and sent across the river abundance of grain. It so happened that three years thereafter Chin was suffering from famine, and pleaded with Tsin for help. Tsin adopted the unanimous advice of his ministers to attack Chin while helpless from lack of food. When the heavy rain of late autumn had converted the land into deep mud in which the chariots sank to the hub, Tsin crossed the river and surrounded the Chin army. The duke was wounded, and the hunger-bitten soldiers were hard pressed, when a sudden attack was made on the Tsin forces with such fury that they were compelled to retreat.

Before that time, the choice horses of Chin were grazing on Mount Ki. A lot of wild men, numbering about three hundred, seized, killed, and were in the act of eating these horses when they were caught and brought before the duke, who was urged to put them to death. He replied that it was commonly said that it was unhealthy to eat horse flesh raw without some spirits to drink with it. This drink he ordered for the hungry men. The thieves were from the neighbourhood and were probably of his own kin. Their gratitude was unbounded, and they offered to become his soldiers. As he was on the point of being overwhelmed by Tsin, they appeared to help their benefactor. So impetuous was their attack, and unexpected, that not only was the duke delivered, but the ruler of Tsin was made prisoner. In the following winter he was liberated and sent to his own capital. This generosity he repaid by handing over to Chin all the lands belonging to him on the west side of the river.

CONFUCIUS.   LAOTZU.

Then for the first time did the frontier of Chin touch the Yellow River. The duke, in his thirty-third year, attacked Tsin, and was so completely defeated that, to save himself, he fled to the Yung, whose chief sent him home under the escort of Yow Hu, a man who had fled to the Yung from Tsin. To him the duke expatiated on the palaces, houses, and stores which he had prepared after Chinese style. When the inspection was over, Hu said that the care of looking after these things was a heavy burden. At this sentiment the duke expressed surprise, and said, " The Middle Kingdom possesses the Odes, the History, Ceremonial, and Laws to conduct the Government, yet there is lawlessness. How without these can the Yung guide their State ? " Hu laughed and said, " Those books and regulations are the root out of which have grown the troubles of China. Through them the superiors rule and domineer over the inferiors, who repay with a spirit of envy and revenge. Thus the classes are mutually opposed. The Yung are different. Superiors treat inferiors with gentleness and virtue, inferiors serve superiors with faithfulness and truth. Thus the entire nation is like one body." Hu was invited to a feast, at which he was plied with questions on the political position of the Yung. It transpired that the Chief was indolent, and paid little attention to public business. Hu remained in the service of Chin. He was afterwards employed by Chin to attack the Yung, whom he drove westward a thousand li. When this duke died, one hundred and seventy-seven men were slain to follow him. Among them were three of conspicuous ability, deeply mourned by the people. To express their grief, an Ode was composed, which is still extant.

Mencius stated that by accepting the guidance of a Chinese Councillor, Duke Mu became the greatest prince of his day. Of his forty sons, the oldest became Duke Kang (621). During his reign of twelve years, a condition of constant war prevailed between him and Tsin. Though victory varied, the battlefield was always on the soil of Tsin.

In the time of Duke Whi (500), Confucius was wandering over the state of Lu. In the twelfth year of his successor, Confucius died. In the twenty-fourth year of the reign of Li Chi, who began his reign in 476, the people of Tsin murdered their ruler, and the state was divided between the three states of Wei, Han, and Chao. Strife including murder in the reigning family of Chin produced anarchy, which terminated only in 415, under Duke Chien, who introduced the wearing of the sword.

Duke Hien began to reign in 385. He abolished the custom

of putting men to death to follow the dead. He erected a new
capital at Liyang. He died after a reign of twenty-four
years, throughout which war was incessant, and many scores
of thousands of men were slain. His son Hiao succeeded in
361. China east of the river was then broken into six large
and twelve small kingdoms. Chin was outside these. Its
neighbour to the south was Chu, and across the river was
Wei, which had absorbed Tsin. Wei began to build the Great
Wall, to protect the land from the incursions of the Huns to
his north.

In his third year, one Yang from Wei was employed at
court. He recommended improvement of the laws, greater
attention to laws, a code of punishment, and the adoption of
rewards and punishments, by which soldiers would be stimulated to fight to the death. The recommendations were ap-
proved by the duke, opposed by the officials, and resented by
the people, who, after experiencing the improvements effected
in three years, changed their minds, called him a great leader,
and all but worshipped him. The duke erected a new capital
at Hienyang, where he set up a recording office, in which to
preserve a history of the kingdom. He began the concentration
of the people into large centres, which he called HIEN, of which
there were forty-one, each with 12,500 families, under an
official called Ling. Roads were made from west to east,
and from north to south. Fields were carefully marked off
with boundaries. He instituted levies for the army, and
changed the method of taxation. For all these improvements
he was made a Count. He died in the twenty-fifth year of
his reign, throughout which Yang proved himself a great
warrior. His son, prince Whi Wen, succeeded him, and
immediately put Yang to death. When Yang was introducing
his new methods, the heir had declared that he would not
submit to them. Yang retorted that the law must be obeyed.
If the heir disobeyed he would be the first to feel the severity
of the law. The heir set up a royal family establishment,
every member of which hated Yang. As soon as the heir became Count, Yang was put to death. The Count was soon
made a Wang, or Prince. In his twelfth year he instituted a
royal hunt, like his suzerain. He changed his fourteenth year
into the first of a royal style, in the fifth of which he marched

north to the bank of the river at Lingchia chow, where he touched the river for the first time. From the beginning of his reign there was a state of intermittent war with Wei, in which large numbers were slaughtered on many battlefields, and in taking numerous cities. He defeated with fearful slaughter a combined army of five states, augmented by Hun troops. He took Taiyuen, the capital of Chao, overran Shu in the south, assisted Wei against Yen, made his power felt in all directions, and died the first Prince of his house.

Prince Wu succeeded. The representatives of five great States called to pay their respects. He appointed two Councillors—Left and Right. After great successes in war, he died.

Prince Wu had married a lady of Wei, who was queen but had no son. The son of a woman of Chu was nominated heir. He was a hostage at the Court of Yen. At his father's death he was escorted home. He became prince Chao Siang. A comet appeared in his second year, and great trouble fell on the royal house. The high officials, the royal family, the feudal princes, were put to death as rebels. The widows of preceding rulers were slain or fled. War was continuous. Chao was incorporated into Chin, after losing 400,000 men. The power of Chin had become so unquestioned that the weak lord of Chow, suzerain of all the States, sent to him the nine tripods which had been fashioned at the beginning of the Chow dynasty as emblematic of the entire empire. The owner of the tripods was acknowledged lord of the land. This prince died in 251, the fifty-sixth year of his reign.

Prince Chwang Siang followed in 249, and proclaimed a general amnesty, but war raged against those States which refused to acknowledge him. In the twenty-sixth year of his reign he assumed the title of CHIN SHI WHANG, the first emperor of the Chin dynasty. He extended the bounds and consolidated the power of the empire, established a central government, and unwittingly laid the foundation of a homogeneous people. He professed and practised a creed which reversed the ideals taught by previous thinkers and professed by preceding dynasties. His creed was the rule of physical force now so prominently to the fore in Europe. Centuries of fighting by his family had secured for him the throne. The sharp edge of a sword, always naked, laid the foundation

CARRIAGE OF CONFUCIUS.

村宮即車冠
敬疋南者

of a dynasty, which, by the same method, was to live for a thousand years. He died after a reign of thirteen years. A stormy reign of two years killed his son and terminated his dynasty. Such is the brief outline of the origin and rise of the Chin dynasty, after whom China is probably named.

From this summary the various steps in the rise of the dynasty may be gleaned. Feitsu, the founder, lived at no great distance from the original home of the Chow. He was so notably successful in feeding horses and cattle that the king of Chow ordered him to take charge of the royal horses and cattle. The king was so charmed with the progress of his beasts that he made Feitsu Superintendent of Horse. In 897 B.C. he gifted him an estate which he called Chin, giving himself the clan name of Ying. Both names referred apparently to successful cattle feeding. For generations he and his successors tended the royal herds. All the records testify to the conclusion that he was a member of the nomadic aborigines, whose entire wealth consisted of cattle, horses, and sheep. The "Epitome of History" states that Chin originated on the south of the Yen River, in the north of Shensi, somewhat to the north of the home of Chow. The two great families sprang from the same race. For five centuries Chin continued in friendly relations with their royal patrons, who had treated them with generosity.

The surrounding nomads, designated Yung, from whom the Chin had sprung, continued their old life, as their descendants, the Ordos, do to this day. They sometimes acknowledged, sometimes defied, the royal authority. History relates that when the sovereign ruled well, the barbarians were peaceable, but rebellious when the rule was bad. The reason for this is understood when we reflect that the sovereign, solicitous for the well-being of his subjects, took care that their frontier was suitably guarded. When the aim of his life was private pleasure his subjects were neglected. The nomads attacked only when a chance of success presented itself.

Chin Chung received a new rank, which entitled him to set up a more ceremonious style than his fathers could assume. He procured a chariot and horses, and adopted to a limited extent the ceremonial and music of Chinese States. He was killed while preparing to discharge the commission entrusted to him. His sons were more successful. The Yung were driven out of the Chin home, and the victor was rewarded by a higher Chinese rank. After the lapse of another half century, Duke Siang escorted the new king Ping from the neighbourhood of the terrible Yung to a new capital in the extreme eastern end of the empire. For this he was created a Prince, and became entitled to use the complete Ceremonial of the Chinese. Being barbarians, his forefathers could not use Chinese etiquette. He provided a princely chariot, erected an altar to Shangti on which he offered sacrifices by which he could proclaim his rank to the world. He was authorised to seize all the lands formerly the kingdom of Chow, which, according to Mencius, were a hundred li square. This fact, together with the frequency with which one capital was abandoned, and the facility with which another was erected, shows the small extent of the kingdom, and the poverty of the people at that stage of history.

Under the guidance of Confucius, we must concede to King Wen the possession of much wisdom and great learning. His prison leisure had been devoted to literary research. He mastered the rude characters which did at that time exist in the Shang dynasty. The early Chow made considerable additions to Chinese script. Knowledge of it became general under the authority exercised by the central government. The various States, at the head of which were members of the family or relatives, perceived the utility of this script, and adopted its use. But the relaxation of the central authority tempted these States to assume a semi-independent position. They saw fit to adopt each its own special style. Old characters received a new meaning, some were modified in writing, others were disused and more invented. The writing of Chinese became confused, and was no longer universally intelligible. This literary anarchy was remedied a century before the Chin became a state. One systematic style was promulgated, though it was still limited in extent.

Up to this point, Chin was outwith China. In its semi-barbarian condition its affairs were of so trifling a nature that they did not require a system of writing. But when it became a State under a prince, its affairs were of permanent importance. A Writer was therefore appointed in 750 to record national affairs. From this date literature was studied, and the " people became greatly civilised." The backwardness of Chin civilisation may be inferred not only from its lack of letters, but from the fact that prisons were then established for the first time, and a set of simple laws was drawn up. Even then the kingdom consisted of but a portion of the original Chow west of the river. The stimulus of the new civilising influences produced a greater cohesiveness in the people, which enabled them to drive the Yung beyond all the lands

DISCIPLES OF CONFUCIUS.

formerly belonging to Chow. The lands of Ki and Feng were attached to Chin. A place of sepulture for their deceased rulers was selected.

At the death of Duke Wu, the practice was introduced of killing men to accompany the deceased ruler. For that purpose sixty-six men were killed, and at the death of Duke Mu the number was one hundred and seventy-seven. The practice continued for three centuries, till a ruler arose who abolished it. Among the purely Chinese dynasties there is no trace of this barbarous practice, but it continued to exist among the Huns and the Kitan in Manchuria centuries after the extinction of the Chin dynasty. Now the Kitan, from whom comes the Russian name for China, were descended from the same race as the Chin and Chow. Probably the practice of burning paper money, horses, houses, etc., is a reminiscence of the ancient barbarism.

For many centuries the kingdom of Chin was confined to the ancient home of Chow. Kingdom after kingdom, west, north, and south of them was annexed. When Mu crossed the river eastwards, it was noted as a memorable event. Gradually the whole province of Shensi, which had never in its entirety been connected with Chow, was absorbed by Chin. Before they crossed the river eastward, their kingdom west of the river was considerably larger than was ever that of Chow.

Yet even with their much enlarged country, they still failed to attain the amount of civilisation which the Chinese had acquired. The story of famine relief by Chin in 652 inplies that whether they still retained the cattle-feeding habits of their ancestors or not, they did to a certain extent cultivate the ground. That cultivation was, however, both limited and rude, for, among the radical innovations recommended by the Chinaman Yang in 359, that of agriculture was the most important. His recommendations were adopted, with the result that land became more valuable, necessitating steps for the more exact definition of the boundaries of each man's farm. This of itself was evidence of a higher social order.

The laws were lax, and military discipline far from strict. Under the instructions of Yang, these defects were remedied. Up to that period every new ruler set up a new capital, evidence of the flimsy nature of the buildings, which could be so lightly abandoned and replaced so easily. The various capitals were all in the neighbourhood of Ki, and west of the river. With the concentration of the people, this frequent change of capital became impossible. By the more intelligent attention to agriculture, the more detailed and exact laws, the tightening of social ties, the stricter discipline, the progress

of the State became more rapid. The complete adoption of
Chinese methods, wedding discipline to the natural hardihood
of the Chin people, formed the source of that power which was
able so speedily to annex State after State, till the whole
empire of China was absorbed. From that point there was no
resilience.

In the nomadic condition of life, literature is of little
practical importance. To an agricultural life, settled homes,
cities, and the diversified needs and possessions of a growing
civilisation, written deeds and accounts are indispensable.
A Writer was required in 750 to record important events. A
Councillor was appointed in 697. A Recording Office was
established in 350. Additional learned officials were super-
added as the State increased in extent and influence. The
nomadic races occupying the north of Shansi, the west of
Shensi, the east of Szuchen, were all incorporated in the kingdom of Chin. Those regions with their inhabitants became
a part of the Chinese empire, when Chin Shi Whang took his
seat on the Dragon Throne. By Chin the process of converting
nomads into agriculturists, begun by Chow, was much extended. Additional millions of barbarians became civilised
Chinese. A large proportion of the cities of north-west China
retain now one syllable which was the name of the barbaric
kingdom in that locality when Chin took possession. From
the history of the Chin dynasty we are driven to the conclusion
derived from the history of Chow. And the history of both is
clear evidence of the manner in which the earliest forms of
Chinese civilisation may have been self evolved. The history of
Manchuria for the past three thousand years unfolds repeated
examples of barbaric peoples elevated to the highest forms of
contemporary civilisation by individuals of their own number
who had wisdom and force of character sufficient to adopt,
and to lead others to adopt, agricultural pursuits and a
settled home.

CHAPTER V.

HAN DYNASTY.

The Chow and Chin dynasties of barbarian origin intro-duced millions of non-Chinese among the Chinese people, with whom they became so perfectly united that there is traceable no greater distinction than there exists among the different peoples in Britain or any other European nation. Yet the work of the dynasty of Han in this respect is greater than all that went before. This dynasty was purely Chinese, and sprang up in the neighbourhood of the cradle of the Chinese civilisation.

East of the city of Kaifeng fu is a small city, Tangshan hien. North of this town is Mangshan hien. Between the two stretches an extensive swamp on the west side of Feng hien. Near Feng is a town, Pei hien, where was born, in the beginning of the Chin dynasty, one Liw Pang. His occupation was that of keeper of a lodging-house near the swamp. Lodging-houses at a distance of three and a-half miles apart, had been planted by Chin Shi Whang all over the empire. They were prepared for the accommodation of travellers, but the keeper had to take note of the character of the inmates. When the times were so much out of joint, disbanded soldiers and rest-less young men found roving and robbing the easiest and most profitable kind of life.

Liw Pang was a tall man, well proportioned, with a promi-nent nose. He loved humanity, and delighted in deeds of charity. He was of comprehensive mind, and penetrating judgment. He would not selfishly provide by partiality undue wealth for his relatives. An official perceiving his re-markable physiognomy and figure, gave him his daughter to wife. An important part of his duty was to guide travellers who desired to go to Lishan, where was an imperial tomb. Those who ventured to go alone were in danger of getting lost in the swamp. They went usually into his booth and had a rest and a drink.

On one occasion, when a number of rowdies had gradually collected, Liw said that those who wished to cross the swamp should go all together, and he would conduct them. He gave them liberally to drink, and while it was yet dark about a dozen volunteered to go under his guidance. When they were mid-way across they found a great serpent lying athwart the narrow path. Liw drew his sword and beheaded it. Immediately an old woman wailed and cried, " My son, the son of the white emperor, who had been changed into a serpent, has been killed by the son of the red emperor." She disappeared suddenly.

In the ninth moon of the year 209 B.C., Liw assumed the title of duke of Pei. China, in its hatred of the Chin rule, was in disorder. About twenty " kingdoms " struggled for existence and ultimate dominion. A Chin force sent against Liw was defeated. In the first moon of 208, Chang Liang was leading a band of over a hundred young men to join the king of Chu, who was living not far from Pei. While on the road he encountered Duke Pei, who engaged him as an officer. They went to the King, who engaged Pei to fight Chin. He was defeated, but took the city of Tang, whose garrison of 6000 men joined him. Though he now commanded 9000 men, he failed in an attack on Feng.

Duke Pei continued fighting. In the spring of 207 he was joined by Peng Yu, who had been a fisherman in the swamp. Several hundred young men had united to call him leader. They were undisciplined, and many hung back when engaged in fight. He told them that those who held back were too many to kill, but he would note the last man and put him to death. They all laughed, but he kept his word. The hindmost man was killed. The men were afraid, and henceforth obedient. Over a thousand wandering soldiers joined him, and the entire company went over to Pei. In the autumn the governor of Nanyang city revolted to Pei, who entered the pass of Wukwan. Just then the Chin emperor was murdered by one of his own officials. Later, Pei took Lantien kuan, a place fortified by Chin Shi Whang, in the neighbourhood of Lantien hien.

In the winter of 206, when Pei was at Pashang, a few miles east of Changan, the young emperor of Chin submitted and presented to him the imperial sceptre and regalia. On entering

Hienyang, the capital of Chin, he was astonished at the splendour of the city, its palaces, and precious furnishings. To prevent looting, he sent his army back to Pashang. His thoughtfulness greatly delighted the people, as did his proclamation that he would treat them all as his own people. Their joy was boundless. They brought unlimited supplies of oxen, sheep, all sorts of edibles and spirits. He refused to accept the style of Prince Chin, but adopted that of Prince Han. He nominated princes for the various States, even for those which had given no sign of adhesion. His principal officials were notable scholars, and when he returned to Loyang he was welcomed by the officials there, as one victorious because of his virtue. Confucianism was permitted again to speak. Next year he set up a temple dedicated to Ancestors, and another for Land and Grain. In his fourth year he was still in Loyang capital, after several campaigns against the States still opposing him. In the following year he assumed the title of Emperor Han. This was in B.C. 202. Next year he proclaimed an amnesty, having disbanded his soldiers, and sent them to their homes and farms.

Throughout the course of their history, Chin had been in a state of war with the Yung and the Ti on all sides of them, who had at that time adopted the name of Huns. Those of them who chose the gipsy life of their forefathers retired westwards and north beyond the Yellow River. With the change of dynasty they mustered courage to march southwards across the river to the land of their fathers, which had become occupied by farmers. From that time forward for many years they were constantly attacking or attacked. They frequently inflicted and often suffered terrible losses. Their power to inflict serious injury was great as long as the Han emperor was securing order in China proper. With the completion of this duty, he was able to pay more attention to his western and northern frontiers.

His capital in Loyang was in the eastern extremity of the empire, and far from the centre of disturbance by the nomads. In B.C. 199 he visited Changan, and resolved to make it the capital. It was a small town, not far removed from Hienyang, the capital of the late dynasty, and situated in the south-east corner of the former kingdom of both Chow and Chin. He

D

died before accomplishing his design. His successor, to the
great satisfaction of the people, devoted himself to breaking
up unoccupied lands around Changan. In 193 he had completed the north-west portion of the fort of Changan. The
great city was completed in B.C. 190. It was selected, doubt-
less, because of its vicinity to the sources of greatest disturbance. Many years of fighting were occupied in breaking
the power of the Huns ; but this was at length successfully
accomplished. The Huns moved westwards into central Asia,
whence in due course they were a disturbing element for
centuries in western Asia and eastern Europe.

In that prolonged warfare the armies of Han penetrated
into central Asia. Traces of this irruption of the Chinese into
the remote west were found by Stein in Khotan. It is important to note that this was the first time in which Chinese
found their way so far to the west.

During the Han dynasty the provinces of Kansu and Szu-
chuen on the west, those of Chihli and Manchuria on the north,
those of Shantung and the sea-coast on the east, were absorbed into the government of China. Ultimately the Yangtsu was crossed, and the boundaries of China proper were made
practically what they are to-day. Many of the inhabitants
of those widely spread regions chose to retain the social condition in which they and their fathers had lived. Many fled
north and west ; many retired into the mountains separating
the various provinces along the north, the west, and the
south of China.

But most preferred to remain in the country with which
they were familiar, and submitted to Chinese dominion.
They adopted the speech, customs, and modes of life of the
Chinese, were numbered with and soon became indistinguishable from them. The lands on the south-east and
across the Yangtsu adopted Chinese dress, education, literature, customs, and mode of life, while remaining differentiated
in speech.

From what is recorded of the Mythical Ages, of the Chow,
the Chin, and the Han dynasties, we are justified in concluding that the Chinese people are autochthonous, and their
civilisation indigenous. With the expeditions of the Han to
the west, we come in touch with the first reference to contact

by the Chinese with any people west of the Yellow River, other than their nomadic neighbours.

It is true that at a remarkably early period of their history, they were under the influence of a clear and practical belief in One Supreme Ruler who reigned over heaven and earth and all things.* The harmonious motions of the worlds above, the wonderful manifestations and infinite forms of life on earth, with their marvellous adaptations, appealed to the same mental powers in eastern China as they did in western Asia, or in eastern Europe. The harmony could exist only from Unity, the existence of visible forces and their control implied Power irresistible, and despite the wild theories of ancient or of modern times, the mind of normal humanity must find a cause in perfect wisdom for the concurrence of means with ends, so apparent in the countless forms of adaptation.

The Chinese were, therefore, not a homogeneous race. They were not descended from an unmixed race. Hundreds of barbarian kingdoms, as conquerors or as conquered, came under the moulding influence of the tiny Middle Kingdom, which was born in, and developed from, the north-east corner of Honan.

Yet more remarkable than would be the homogeneity of race is the mental homogeneity of the people. Though in their racial origin and their physical constitution they are an amalgam of a score of nationalities, they resent the notion that they are not one race. They read the same books ; they perform practically the same ceremonial ; they affect the same religion ; they think the same thoughts. To the world at large they are an indivisible people. The manner in which the Boxer madness spread over the entire land affected every class of society, and but for a few men, would have involved every province and every hamlet in the clamour for the blood of the foreigner—demonstrated to all the world the solidarity of the Chinese people.

---

* See " Original Religion of China."

CHAPTER VI.

OBJECTIONS.

It may be objected that both the physique and the speech of the Chinese militate against the above theory. With little differences in height the Chinese appear to be all alike, and though there are dialects in their speech, it seems practically the same everywhere. These two points require consideration.

When travelling to China across America, our train was stopped near a hill on a Sunday in June 1872. The sun was brilliant, and the day one of perfect calm. We pulled up before the farthest west town east of the Rockies. On the preceding day a waterspout had washed down a hillside. Rocks, trees, and earth covered the railway track for miles to the depth of several feet. Till this debris should be cleared away we were prisoners. After some hours it was reported that several Chinese had arrived from Sacramento to clear the road. Another gentleman and myself walked up the line to see the kind of people to whom I was going out as missionary. Several small groups were passed of boys, all working as though they were machines like the spades they wielded. At length we encountered a tall man of the western race. We inquired where the Chinese men were, as we had seen nothing but boys. " That's all we've got for men," was the reply, in a good Irish brogue. The discovery that the Chinese were so puny a race was a disappointment. In Yokohama we came across Chinese again. They were tall, handsome, well-dressed, and with a smart, keen air went about all business places, banks, customs, wherever there were transactions involving money or valuables. Instead of the down-trodden look of the coolies, they moved about with erect head as though they were masters of the place. They were all of good medium height, lithe, active young men. The impression made east of the Rockies was obliterated.

Even the cursory glance of the passing traveller cannot fail to note the difference between the physique of the people of the south and those of the north. The regions south of the Yangtsu and those on the east coast were annexed to China immediately before and after the beginning of the Christian era. The people of those regions are not the same race as the Chinese. They are a small people. From them went the boys whom we saw on the American railway. Their kindred are still to be found among the wild mountains between the various southern provinces, where they lead a more or less independent life. The southern Chinese have for twenty centuries been living a life mentally and physically different from the hillmen, who have retained the habits of their ancient forefathers. They became Chinese by education.

The inhabitants of the Yellow River region are of a totally different race. They belong to the tall races, as are the people inhabiting Mongolia and Manchuria. The difference in physique of Mongol and Chinese is explicable by their different mental and physical pursuits. They differ more in facial outline and expression. Chinese are agricultural, and by their strenuous life develop their muscles and bodily energies to the utmost. The nomadic races lead a sedentary life, their most violent exercise being on horseback. These diverse bodily exercises in the course of generations produce facial changes. Labour in a vitiated atmosphere deteriorates the bodies of those who come from the country. Health and proper development depend largely on the location and nature of one's occupation. But more especially is life intellectual and literary, influential in modifying facial development. As in Europe so in north China, facial differences are the product of similar causes. Confining attention to these facts, the physique of the peoples of at least north China points naturally to the conclusion that they are fundamentally one.

Diverse customs and differing languages do undoubtedly point to another conclusion. Asia displays a general uniformity in style of dress. The long, loose robe of dignified leisure is all but universal. Variety in details of shape or ornamentation are accounted for by difference in climate, of education, of taste, so that the style of clothing is no criterion whereby to decide differences of race. Even now the Chinese are changing the style of their costume, on account of changes introduced into their mode of life.

Speech presents a more difficult problem. Yet the condition of the South Sea Islands proves that speech, when free from the trammels of letters, is capable of undergoing great changes. To the changes in the South Sea Islands there is a close analogy in the south of China, where the verbiage and pronunciation differ so materially from those of the north that they have not been reduced to Chinese writing. But the language in the neighbourhood of the Yellow River has been uniform. The idiom, the grammar, the verbiage have continued practically the same from ancient ages. A change has been introduced lately into the pronunciation. Throughout the whole of north China it was formerly what it is now in Shantung, where the pronunciation of the Ming dynasty is retained. The Manchus have exercised a softening influence, which has produced the Pekinese dialect. By the Manchu and other northern officials, who spread themselves over the country, that pronunciation has diffused itself over many parts of south China. But notwithstanding such modification in pronunciation, the written form has prevented any radical divergence from the ancient language.

Now this language differs essentially from those of the nomads, who in all directions speak a language similar in construction to Mongol or Turkish. How, then, could the Chinese people be composed largely of transformed nomads whose posterity possess no trace of their ancestral polysyllabic tongue ? A probable explanation can be found in the present condition of China.

The Manchus, who lived for centuries in the game-stocked valleys east of Mukden, spoke a polysyllabic language, possessing neither alphabet nor literature. They and the Koreans are traceable to a common ancestry who in the remote past inhabited part of northern Manchuria. With the lapse of centuries, their languages have become absolutely distinct, while both are essentially different from Chinese. Like that of the Mongols, both are polysyllabic and Turanian. When the Manchus entered China they possessed a language reduced to writing by the adaptation of Mongol letters. Their power raised their language to a place of honour. Their pride of conquest made it natural to retain in their language the evidence of their racial bravery. They took measures to make that language an official and a classical one. Dictionaries were prepared and other books, whereby Chinese could learn Manchu and Manchus preserve their own tongue. Schools were established, and able teachers appointed. By a generous liberality in the employment of these methods, they perfected their language, making it highly respectable and thoroughly grammatical. They had every inducement to keep themselves apart as a people. They adopted whatever forms of literature tended to secure this design. Every important State document written in Chinese was duplicated in Manchu, and carefully preserved in the Archives. Yet within two centuries the conquering Manchus had forgotten their own national tongue and spoke only the monosyllabic language of the conquered race. A comparatively small number of young Manchus of more than average ability were set apart as writers of Manchu documents. With accuracy and great beauty of penmanship they discharged this duty efficiently. But the speech of even these men was Chinese. With not a few of these scholarly Manchus I was acquainted who could not speak the Manchu language, and who, still more strangely, were unable to pronounce properly some letters of their own original tongue, but pronounced them as Chinese do the same letters of the west.

If Manchus who had every inducement to retain the differentiation afforded by their original language, adopted under moral or social compulsion the Chinese language, literary and spoken, it is not surely difficult to understand how a similar result could arise from circumstances which were much more favourable to such a change.

For three thousand years from the time of Tan Fu, tribes to the north and west of China abandoned their nomadic life for the settled life of the Chinese. The number of nomads who from first to last fell within the circle of Chinese life and influence amounted to many millions. They necessarily occupied an inferior position. This would compel them instinctively to adopt whatever means would most speedily obliterate all traces of their origin, and assimilate them most completely to the Chinese. As the Manchus had serious reasons for the retension of their distinctive language, these nomads

had equally serious reasons to forget theirs. To remain
isolated was the Manchu policy ; to become absorbed in the
main body of the Chinese was that of the nomads. With
avidity they adopted Chinese speech, Chinese education,
Chinese modes of clothing, of preparing and eating food, of
manners and customs. The second generation would be
indistinguishable from the Chinese. When foreigners of any
race as conquerors or as conquered, entered the land of China,
they were speedily assimilated to the Chinese.

CHAPTER VII.

CONCLUSION.

Investigation of the anthropological facts available leads the student to the inference that north-eastern Europe and the high latitudes of Asia were in the remotest known times inhabited by peoples of the Turanian race. The inhabitants of eastern Asia were of kindred race, with the possible exception of the hairy Oinos of northern Manchuria. The peoples of the high latitudes were of the tall nations of the world, as were those of China down to latitude 25°. Farther south the people were of similar type, but of smaller size. They were all of a low stage of civilisation, varying, however, from the rudest savagery to nomadic tent-dwellers. From among these a small community began on the south bank of the Yellow River to cultivate grain in a crude fashion. This life necessitated a permanent abode and personal possessions. Thus and here was the embryonic beginning of China.

From the chapter on the Mythical Age we learn that the Chinese trace their ancestors back to a condition of savagery in pre-historic time. Some made their home in nests on trees to escape the teeth and the venom of wild beasts. Others lived beneath the shade of great pine trees in summer and in deep pits in winter. They ate the seeds of grasses, the kernels of nuts, and the flesh of wild beasts with the hair on. They were ignorant of cooking, for they did not know the use of fire. They lived together promiscuously like the birds and the beasts. They covered their nakedness with the skins of animals slain for food.

Thirty centuries B.C., Fuhi is said to have taken the first step out of that purely animal existence, by the institution of marriage. This implied the division of society into separate families, involving some sort of dwelling. Cloth did not then exist of either cotton or silk. Whether the dwelling was made of the branches of trees, or out of the semi-clayey soil, the story sayeth not.

Compared with that stage of existence, the nomadic tribes exhibit marked superiority. They possessed flocks of sheep, herds of cattle and of horses, of the origin of which there is no record. Their beasts could live only where water was found, and where grass grew. These conditions governed the mode of life of their owners. A permanent place of abode was impossible. A dwelling was provided of woven hair. It was movable, easily erected, and speedily pulled down when water failed or grass was exhausted. This life involved the right to move about in an extensive tract of country, which, however, was strictly limited by the grazing grounds of neighbouring tribes. They came to know the use of fire, by which they smelted metals, and fashioned weapons wherewith to master the lower animals and protect themselves from prowling enemies. They were illiterate, rude, and cruel. These conditions still exist largely in Asia. Their illiteracy was ended by the Nestorians, who also had a hand in modifying their cruelty, along with Buddhism and Mahommedanism.

In that section of the populace which grew into the kingdom of China, one devoted himself to the cultivation of some of the grasses, the seeds of which had been eaten in their wild state. Some varieties of these still grow wild in north China. The attention given to the cultivation of the soil improved the quality of the grasses, and the cultivator established for himself an imperishable name.

The cultivation of the soil necessitated a fixed abode, and produced a more compacted state of society, the various relations of which had to be adjusted so as to secure the peace and smooth existence of the community. As long as all were equally toilers in the fields, life continued simple. Varying degrees of intelligence and diligence resulted in unequal degrees of possessions ; for there is no evidence of communistic life. By the lapse of time and increase of population, the relations of the people became more complicated. Trades and professions rose automatically out of the needs of the people. These were mutually complementary, but their interests were ofttimes antagonistic. The interaction of these various elements gave occasion for the introduction of regulations which became stereotyped into laws. Certain forms of authority were established with power to decide between conflicting claims and interests, and, if need be, to restrain and to punish. To protect their property and lives from surrounding barbarians always ready to plunder, means had to be devised and weapons provided of a more deadly nature than were required to meet the dangers arising from wild beasts or internal troubles.

When men's needs were few and possessions scanty, their affairs could be all trusted to memory. Numerous possessions and varied, demanded a permanent record. Writing appears to have been at first pictorial. Is soon became abbreviated to mere outlines. The outlines of two or more pictures were combined to represent general terms, as the combination of sun and moon to describe brightness, physical or mental. Thus did the art of writing originate.

All these changes took place in the nucleus formed among the savages in north-east Honan, who were the embryo of the Chinese nation. When Yao began to reign in Pingyang, the various departments of a well-regulated state were all in good working order. The people of Yao and their predecessors were the founders of the polity and language of China. In the succeeding generations their descendants increased largely on lands which were very fertile, and in circumstances which were favourable. Yet they could be the parents of not a tithe of the population of the China of to-day. The population of the China of to-day, as to at least nine-tenths of their number, are the descendants of those tribes and kingdoms who, in the time of Yao, were the uncultivated barbarians of the lands all around. Except in the south-east corner of China, there is no evidence visible to the eye of any racial distinction between various parts of the Chinese empire. All are equally the descendants of the same Turanian race, brought at different times under the influence of an indigenous civilisation. We have traced the cradle of the Chinese people and the origin of the race. But the region of the origin of their Turanian predecessors remains an unknown problem.

The late Dr Legge, than whom there has been no greater Chinese scholar, declared at the close of a long life that after his many years' study of Confucius, he could see nothing which would entitle him to be called a great man. Yet the homogenity of so mixed a people as the Chinese is the work of Confucius. The sword had much to do with binding other nations to China with chains, the teaching of Confucianism alone has constituted China a unit. That was the furnace which melted the heterogeneous masses and made them an indivisible whole. They resemble no other nation. The ethics of Confucius constitute their ideal morality. His ceremonial guides their lives. The mutual regulations of society are regulated by his rules. The principles laid down by him for the government of the nation are regarded as infallibly correct, and are continually and universally appealed to. Is there any other system of philosophy or of ethics which can compare in the extent of its influence with Confucianism ? Chin Shi Whang would not have devoted so much expense and energy to unearth and to destroy every scrap of Confucianism had it been merely a system for literary research. Dynasties subsequent to him were wise enough to learn the lesson. Many of them were no better than he, but no one was ever bold enough to make a public confession of his creed, even when following his practice. We see one such in Europe, and see also the outcome. It was to make his system of government the more easily carried out that he took such savage measures to extirpate the ethical teaching of Confucius. His sword was broken in cutting up those books. His name is execrated to this day by the best and most thoughtful minds of China, while that of Confucius is glorified and shall always be held in honour. The teaching which has already raised so large a proportion of mankind from savagery to a high plane of civilisation shall in the future, when imbued with the active spirit of Christianity, raise them still higher for the good of a new China, on which will depend much of the welfare of the world.

SECTION II.—EDUCATION.

CHAPTER I.

THEORY OF EDUCATION.

The value of Confucianism as a method of controlling the
life and guiding the thought of the people has been depreciated
both by Chinese and by foreigners. For this depreciation
one of two possible causes may have been responsible. One
is ignorance of the essential teaching of the system, another is
the contempt for all learning which is not based on physics.
Chin Shi Whang, whose rule was the embodiment of brute
force, exerted his utmost to exterminate Confucianism. He
persecuted to the death those devoted to the system, and
committed to the flames all books containing any portion of
it. This fact of itself affords abundant evidence of the nature
of the teaching. That government based on brute force came
to a speedy close. Resuscitated Confucianism became more
influential as the years glided by. If it has failed to make
China an ideal kingdom, it is because, like Christianity in
Europe, it has never been permitted to exert to its full extent
its proper influence over the private life of the individual, or
the public life of the nation. The correct test of its value is
its adaptability to the mental condition of the people, and
its moral influence upon them. To ennoble them by adapting
itself to their characteristics, the special form of Confucianism
represented by the books now known had its origin and its
prolonged existence. When we reflect that to it the Chinese
largely owe their unique position among the nations, and their
ability to act as teachers to all surrounding Asiatic peoples,
we are driven to conclude that the system contains potent
influences for good, which are worthy of our serious consideration. And further, history proves that it has elevated a
larger number of millions, over a wider area, for a longer

period than any other philosophic system known among mankind. It has been the moral teacher not of China only, but of all the neighbouring countries, every one of which owes to it the best features of their social life and public institutions, both of which would have been much improved by a more thorough devotion to the practical application in ordinary life of the ethical principles of the system. Nor should the fact be overlooked that the observance of those principles, imperfect though it has been, is the main element in the marvellous continuity of the national existence of the Chinese people, and of the comparatively high form of civilisation by which they were enabled to assimilate the huge masses of barbarians who became one with themselves. The theory of education on which that system is based is, therefore, worthy of more examination than it has received.

It is worthy of particular attention that the Confucian philosophy and teaching are based on REVERENCE. They aim at the development of character, and the attainment of real culture, rather than of the knowledge which consists of a mere accumulation of facts. Its intention is to lead the people to become nobler men and better citizens. Confucius and Mencius, the two great teachers, craved for no renown by publishing startling innovations and novel theories. They did not expect riches from their teaching. They had no sect, large or small, to glorify. Their mental activity and bodily labours were laid on the altar of service for their country. They sought to rectify the wrongs in, and establish peace and contentment throughout, their distracted land. Their method was the "instruction which lays out in orderly arrangement the Way which develops to its fullest extent the nature given to man by Heaven." Mencius affirms that humaneness is the heart of man, and integrity his path. He deplores the calamity of him who misses the path and does not desire to regain it ; who loses his heart and does not wish to find it again. Men lose thier fowls and dogs and search for them ; they lose their heart and have no wish to seek for it. The true aim of learning is to find the lost heart. The heart is the disposition given by God to all mankind.

This definition of education points out its sphere and its limitations. Its sphere is the mind of man. Its office is to unfold the talents, the abilities, the feelings and desires in-

herent in the heart or mind, as originally constituted by its
Creator. The work of education is to guide the entire life
in accordance with that original constitution. All speculation
in regard to the beginnings of man or of things, all baseless
theorizings about their nature, all that cannot be the subject
of real knowledge, is rigorously excluded. Human nature as
known to or knowable by man, together with the duties of
human relationships, embrace the entire field and scope of
education. By the development of his original nature, education establishes man's character, and thus fits him to be a
useful member of society, able to discharge all duties devolving on him as a member of the community and a subject
of the State. Ethics and politics were the warp and the
woof of man's life and conduct. The severance of these two
produced disaster to both. This education is practical throughout, labouring solely for the amelioration of the lot of mankind in all its classes and without exception. Statesmen or
rulers who paid no special regard to the public well-being
were unworthy of their position, and should not have been
permitted to occupy it. The ideal which inspired these
teachers was to create a renewed people, a moral nation.
They did not strive to have a set of fine phrases inserted on
the statute book. They sought to change the warped disposi-
tions and renew the aberrant heart of men. They desired to
produce men whose goodness would, by the influence of their
example, change or modify the wickedness of a nation. The
man properly educated became the noble man. His character was stable, so that he could be universally trusted. He
would die rather than offend against the right. His knowledge was full and clear on the facts and principles bearing
on the life of man in all his relationships. He was the man
of culture who knew how to live his life faultlessly and thus
show to others the way in which they ought to go.

By instruction, Confucius did not mean literary accomplish-
ments exclusively. Though the knowledge which produced
culture was his chief, it was not his sole object. Passing
through the kingdom of Wei, a disciple drew his attention
to the density of the population, and asked, " What should be
done for them ? " " Enrich them," was the answer. " And
what after that ? " " Instruct them in letters," he said. On
another occasion he said that ceremonial and ritual are sub

sequént to the acquisition of the necessaries of life, as painting in colour follows the preparation of the plain and solid surface on which the painting is done. A young man should learn to be filial in his own house, and respectful to the seniors he meets. He should be sincere in his conduct and diligent in his business. After these primary duties are fulfilled, he should devote himself to the study of literature. Thus, though demanding first the solid qualities of character and the physical necessities of life, he was no less insistant on the claims of culture. According to his own figure, if the plain ground is prepared, it is necessary for perfection that colour be superimposed.

To attain a cultured mind, two lines of study are indispensable. First comes the study of words, and then that of literature. The use of words is to express clearly to the hearer what is in the mind of the speaker. If his definition differs from that of the astute French statesman, it is because he was a teacher whose aim in the use of words was to make his meaning clear, while the statesman sought to hide his meaning in a cloud of words, as the cuttlefish hides in its own sepia. Words, therefore, or names, should be perfectly understood by the speaker, and used with such accuracy as to prevent any misunderstanding in the hearer. The first requisite in good government is the correct use of names, so that speech cannot mislead the hearer. If speech be misleading, affairs cannot be properly conducted, the proprieties, politeness, and music cannot flourish, punishment cannot be justly administered. All this breeds uncertainty in the minds of the people, who know not how to act. The art of government consists in the correct use of words. When the father is father and the son is son, each knows and executes his own proper duties.

Next to the correct use of words comes the study of literature, by which can be unlocked the treasury wherein repose the intellectual and moral jewels of former generations. Of the extant literature he regarded the Odes as pre-eminent. He recommended his only son to study them, because without a knowledge of the Odes he was not worth talking to. Students of special ability were put to study the Odes, because these stimulated the mind, explained the nature of sociability, and the occasions when anger was justifiable. They teach how to serve one's parents in private life, and one's sovereign in public. They give the names of beasts, birds, and plants. Politeness came next to the Odes, for knowledge of it made one's character stable. He lectured much on the Odes, the Book of History, the duties of propriety and politeness. The chief burden of his lectures was, however, letters, conduct, faithfulness, and truth, the two last being the foundation of his system. He lectured frequently on Human Nature and the Way of Heaven, which his students were unable to understand. A very few fragments remain, which were memorable on account of their special application.

Each line of study was supposed to produce its own specific influence on the character. Study of the Odes was calculated to improve the stupid, of History to correct error, of Music to prevent extravagance. The Yiking counteracted the tendency to incur risks. Propriety is the antidote to worry and annoyance ; and a knowledge of the Spring and Autumn Annals would prevent social disorder.

Self-cultivation should be the aim of every one, beginning with the sovereign. This forms the root of all culture, no part of which can flourish if it be neglected. The Great Learning was prepared to publish notable virtue. It teaches how a people can be renewed in character, how they can attain the perfection of virtue, with anything short of which they should not be satisfied. It sets forth that Heaven is the source of all truth, which cannot be changed, and whose substance is found in the mind, and must not be abandoned. Careful introspection will preserve and nourish it. Self-examination will discover the principles of truth in the mind of the student, and the embodiment of them in practice will make him strong to repel every temptation from without alluring him to selfishness. Acquaintance with the attainments of ancient worthies will stimulate him to do well. He shall thus be guided to the realisation of perfect goodness. Of all this, self-cultivation is the root.

Though the form of teaching differs from, and its design, scope, and limits bear striking resemblance to, those of the teachings of Socrates a century later, in both systems good conduct is represented as the outcome of knowledge, and evil as the fruit of ignorance. The wise acquire knowledge, and know-

E

ledge increases wisdom. Knowledge is one with wisdom,
and is the result of study and learning. The wise are therefore students not for a few years at school, but for life. While
retaining with firm grip all the knowledge already possessed,
they add continuously to their stock. This ceaseless learning
increases their knowledge, their knowledge enlarges their
wisdom, and their wisdom guides them into a growingly nobler
and higher, because a more useful, life. Adequate knowledge
will prevent all forms of evil conduct.

Ignorance being the mother of every kind of evil, the first
duty of education is to teach each man his ignorance. True
knowledge is to know when you know, and to know when you
do not know. When one is able to teach others clearly, it is
evidence that he knows his subject. To know in a general
way is ignorance. If the extent of one's culture does not fully
reach up to the level of his original talents, the result is rudeness ; if one's culture is in excess of those talents, he becomes
puffed up with affectation. When culture and talents blend
in proper proportions, the result is the noble man.

But mere knowledge is not sufficient. Admiration for excellent precepts is of no practical use without the application
of them to the reformation of character. There is little hope
of the man who expresses delight in fine sentiments, but who
fails to guide the actions of his life by them. Learning was
essential to the production of a well-balanced mind. Without
it there are six excellences of character which become degraded
into vices. The love of humaneness degenerates into stupid
simplicity, the love of knowledge leads to mental dissipation,
the resolve to be truthful begets recklessness, the determination
to be straight results in rudeness, the love of bravery becomes
insubordination, and the man who will be firm is insolent.

Confucius and Plato were of one mind in regarding education to be vitally important as a means of securing the safety
of the State and the well-being of the individual. In the
system of Confucius there was no place for class distinctions.
There were no helots in China. The benefits of education
were accessible to every member of the community capable of
receiving them. The system was absolutely democratic.
Confucius accepted students of all ranks and conditions. He
took fees, but would not turn away the young man who could

present only a bundle of dried fish. He selected his students by tests of his own, rigorously applied. These tests were not based on rank or wealth or previous knowledge, nor did he seek any certificate of character. His test was based on the natural abilities and diligence of the student. He took the student on his own professions, and speedily discovered his characteristics. Those who passed his test were all taught in the same fashion. It so happened that the poorest of them, who could barely clothe himself, and who lived on the very edge of want, was held up by him as an example to others, both for quickness of apprehension and for readiness to apply to practise what he had learned. He gave no guarantee to any, but imparted his instruction with equal earnestness to all.

It was his wish to have as students men of exceptionally good life, but he had to deplore the difficulty of finding such as could perfectly observe the " mean." Next to these he desiderated those who, on the other hand, were ardent, or who, on the other, were cautious. The ardent would push ahead, the cautious would fall into no error. The scholar should be earnest and eager among his friends, bland and kindly among his brethren. A high standard of intellect was indispensable. To those who manifested no eagerness he would not expound his doctrines. " If, when I unfold one corner of my subject, my hearer fails to infer the other three, I do not repeat my lesson. To men of a superior mind, subjects of a high order may be expounded ; to men of inferior capacities, they may not."

Mencius was asked how he could accept as students men of whose past life he was ignorant. He replied that there was no man who had not in his heart an antipathy to some kind of wrong. If that man be so trained that he learn to apply that antipathy to other forms of evil which he had tolerated, the result would be humaneness. He who is taught to apply to his entire life his wish to abstain from some forms of injurious conduct, will learn to exercise an all-embracing integrity. His philosophical hypothesis was that whatever be the character of a man at a given time, he had originally a good nature. However battered and torn that nature may have become by evil conduct, it always retains at bottom a permanent appreciation of that which is good. It is therefore

possible to lead him back to the right, however far he may
have wandered in the way of error. He could therefore, with
a clear conscience, admit into his company all sorts of men
irrespective of their past, with the assurance that under his
instruction the original good nature would re-assert itself. He
was optimistic, not because he had found all men good, but
because he believed in the possibility of all men becoming
good.

Intelligence, diligence, and the sincere desire to discover
truth were the qualifications sought in their students by those
great teachers. Their demands were heavy and stringent.
That student who was ashamed of poor food and mean clothing
was not worthy to be taught. He who was always hankering
after comfort was unworthy of the name of student. Study
should be conducted with the anxiety of one stimulated by
dread of failure, or of one afraid to lose what he had already
attained. Good paths are made on the hillside when much
grass is trodden down. But the unused path becomes choked
up with weeds. So does indolence choke up the mind of the
careless student. To learn humaneness demands unfaltering
determination, earnest inquiry, diligent introspection. One
must realise daily what he is lacking, and never forget what
he is capable of doing. To know how to sprinkle and sweep
the floor, to answer questions without hesitation, to acquire
perfectly the way of advancing and retreating gracefully, are
but tiny branchlets of learning. The noble man goes deeply
into it. He makes it the habitation of his mind. He lays hold
of it with both hands, and is eager to attain to perfection, not
only for his own sake, but in order that he may be able to teach
others in brief and simple language. Confucius was a student
so eager in pursuit of knowledge that he forgot his food ; so
joyful over a discovery that he forgot his sorrow ; and so
engrossed in his search that he was unconscious of the ap-
proach of old age.

The acquisition of knowledge is not sudden. Flowing
water advances only after it has filled up the hollows, and the
earnest student progresses step by step. Study also requires
devoted attention. Chess is an art which demands no great
ability. To the instruction on the game by a teacher two men
are listening, one with undivided attention, the other with

a mind distracted by the question how he can set his bow to shoot an approaching swan. The latter will not learn as well as the other. Though continuous effort is indispensable in order to build up the character of the noble man, the result of effort, even when equally constant, is not always the same in all cases. There are differences in the kind of effort ; there are differences in the capacity and the moral character of the students who are equally diligent. Hence will result in the case of every student a difference in the amount of knowledge acquired, in the kind of education, in the influence over mind and life. Sometimes a plant sprouts but does not flower. Sometimes it may produce flowers but grows no fruit. Students may come to be equal to, or even to excel their teachers, but if a man reach forty and do nothing remarkable he is not worthy of respect. The scholar carries a heavy burden over a long way. His burden is the perfection of humaneness. Is it not heavy ? His race is finished only at death. Is it not a long one ? In addition to all this, it must not be forgotten that learning without thinking is waste of energy, and thinking without learning is dangerous.

Only the wise who need not, and the stupid who cannot receive it are incapable of improvement. Some men know truth ; others know and admire, but those are best who know and practise it. Some men are affected by this knowledge like the fertilising influence of seasonable rain. The natural abilities of others are enlarged and developed. The doubts and mental difficulties of others are dissipated. Still others are stimulated to correct and cultivate themselves in private. The wise man desires to acquire all knowledge, but pursues most zealously the most important. He uplifts the virtue of his original nature to its greatest height and widest intelligence, and uses it to spread its greatest possible influence. He can then become the teacher of others. He can cultivate himself in a spirit of reverence, and thus give peace to his neighbourhood, and even extend that peace over the whole empire. Such are the noble men who can observe the mean, and lead others to do likewise. Yet it should be understood that the instructed who do observe the mean, and who refuse to company with those who cannot, are in no real way superior to these. The will of Heaven in producing man is that those who are first to know shall teach those who come after, and that those who understand shall instruct the dull.

Mencius employed various methods of instruction. If he rejected as a pupil one who applied for admission, the very rejection was a method of instructing both the rejected and all who knew of the rejection. To one who asked why he should not modify the demands of his teaching, which, though beautiful and noble, were unpractical as scaling the heavens, he replied that the expert artificer would not change the marking line for the sake of a stupid workman, much less discard it altogether. They will follow who can.

The early dynasties of China regarded the education of the people of prime importance. By means of this education each individual knew his own duties and could perform them. The relation of father and son should be regulated by affection ; of sovereign and minister by faithfulness ; of husband and wife by their relative duties ; of old and young by seniority ; of friends by sincerity. Good government induces fear, good instruction begets love. Good government may obtain the people's wealth, good instruction gains their heart.

It is interesting to compare the state of ancient Greece with that of contemporary China. Confucius was born in 551 B.C., Socrates about 469, Plato in 427, and Mencius in 372. Greece was divided into mutually hostile kingdoms, China into the Fighting Kingdoms. Socrates declared that vice was the product of ignorance, and virtue the fruit of knowledge. It was therefore the duty of every man to acquire intelligent knowledge of himself and of his duties. To stimulate him to learn he must recognise his own ignorance. The philosopher of Plato is the noble man of Confucius. Plato's ideal ruler is absolutely just, and this justice involves the same principles as the humaneness and integrity of the ruler, according to Confucius. Knowledge is good, but its importance lies in its application to the guidance of life. It is never perfect, therefore the search for it persists as long as life endures. Plato attaches most importance to the guidance of the State ; Confucius to the endeavour and example of the individual. The aim of both is one. It is to secure good men and citizens in a well ordered State. This aim is attainable by such an education as shall clearly display the wickedness of all selfish vice, and the excellence of all goodness. When men clearly understand the difference, they shall voluntarily forsake the evil and do the good.

There has never been any religious difficulty to clog the wheels of the educational chariot in China. Only among Europeans have the Chinese seen such hindrances. In this, as in some other matters, the Chinese teach us a lesson. It is surely possible to teach in our schools the excellence of a good and pure life, to teach reverence for every person and thing that is noble and worthy, to show the meanness of selfishness and the discord rising inevitably out of all undue self-seeking, to teach the mutual duties of men and women to each other and the State, without dropping into their young minds the corrosive poison of sectarian strife. Considering the nature of the religion with which we have been dowered, the theory of Confucian education should be the goal of ours.

CHAPTER II.

CONFUCIUS, SKETCH OF LIFE.

The student finds it impossible to dissociate Confucius from the character of Chinese civilisation. He refused the title of Sage, claiming to be but a transmitter of the ancient doctrine. King Wen and Duke Chow were universally acknowledged to be Sages. They knew and formulated the Doctrine, but after their death the teaching of it fell into abeyance for six centuries, till Heaven was pleased to call him to propagate it. Though he was no Sage, he and he only represented those two Sages. Subsequent ages have corroborated this estimate of his knowledge and capacity, and have accorded him the name of Sage. He did resuscitate, enlarge, and popularise the Doctrine, and made it a power a hundredfold greater than ever it was. In his hands it became the instrument chiefly responsible for the China of the past two thousand years. His person cannot therefore be ignored.

It does not lie within the scope of the present work to deal exhaustively with all the information existing about him, but it is necessary to attempt a true estimate of his character in some of its outstanding characteristics. This can be done properly only by studying the literature connected with him. This study should be free from the influence of prejudice or preconceived notions, or any bias against himself or religion. The only satisfactory method in which this can be done is by taking the text of the books representing him and make them tell their own tale. Thus can be given an unbiassed judgment, and any conclusions from the text bear their evidence on the face of them.

Not a few writers who might be supposed to investigate all documents, calculated to illustrate the subject, call him an agnostic, and deny him the possession of any religion. Though his politico-ethical system has had to be excluded from this

work, the section following gives evidence as clear as
any reasonable man can desire of his religious nature and
deep piety, and explains how this religion of his came to
be questioned. He was born in the town of Chufu, in Chang-
ping, of the kingdom of Lu, which was in the south-west of
Shantung, east of the Yellow River. His father was an old
man with a grown-up family, when he married a very young
lady that he might have a worthy son. This son was born in
B.C. 551. Soon after his birth his father died, leaving widow
and child in straitened circumstances. The family name
was Kung, whence comes the first syllable of his name. His
own name was Chiw, and he assumed for title Chung-ni. As
a child he was particularly fond of acting. His play consisted in placing sacrificial vessels—*tow* and *tsu*—in their proper
order, and in assuming the attitudes proper to the ceremony
of sacrificing. At the age of fifteen, in 537, he went to school.
Five years thereafter his son, Bai Yi, was born. He was then
made Inspector of Weights and Measures and Overseer of
Cattle. In 522 he went to the capital, where he is supposed
to have seen Laotsu. That same year he returned to Lu,
which in 517 was thrown into confusion. The Duke was
compelled to flee to the State of Chi, his northern neighbour. Confucius went to the same state. He was offered
a government post which he refused, as he was regarded
with suspicion. He returned to Lu.

Even prior to that date, his scholars had become numerous.
In 509 the Duke was acting so arrogantly that his ministers
rebelled. Confucius refused to accept office. He retired into
private life, and, surrounded by a large number of students,
devoted himself to studying and editing the Odes, History,
Ceremonial, and Music. In 501 he was made Magistrate of
Chungtu, where the reforms initiated by him became so notable that he was promoted to be Minister of Crime. In 498
he was made Director of the Affairs of the Kingdom. Under
the guidance of his counsels the Government soon restored
the country to order. Observing the change in the conditions of Lu, and dreading corresponding personal loss, the
ruler of Chi and his officials devised the plan of sending a
company of beautiful young women with music to the re-
forming Duke. He accepted the gift, and neglected the advice

of his counsellor, who felt conscientiously compelled to resign. He left the country and went to the State of Wei. From this State he intended to go to Chen. On the way he had to pass Kwang, where he was taken for Yang Hu, an oppressor of the people. The people of Kwang threatened him with death. He had to return to Wei, where, in 496, he was invited to meet the famous Nantsu. In the following year he went to the State of Tsao (south-west of Shantung). From Tsao he sought to go to Chen. On this journey, when passing Sung, Whan Tui, who was chief official of that State, threatened to kill him. Three years thereafter he returned to Wei. where Duke Ling was unable to employ him. He was invited to go to the Court of Tsin, but though willing, was prevented by circumstances. He went west to the Yellow River to the State of Chao. Thence he returned to Wei, whose duke sought to gain from him information on the military condition of Chen. This he refused to give, and departed. In 491 he went to Tsai.

Just then the ruler of Lu happened to be seriously unwell. Driving in his chariot, he observed with grief the condition of the city. He said to his son, Kangtsu, that he had the opportunity at one time of making Lu a prosperous city, but had driven away Confucius, whom he now recommended his son to summon as his counsellor. By his advice Lu would certainly become prosperous. When he died his son was unable, from the opposition of the other ministers, to call Confucius to his side, but he invited a disciple, Ran Chiw. This was in 489, and Confucius went to Ke. When he was formerly in Chen he was offered a considerable landed estate if he went to be minister in Chu. He was ready to go, but hearing that serious opposition was offered to the grant of land, he did not go, but went to Wei instead, whose duke had meantime died. His son invited him to remain.

It so happened that just then Ran Chiw had obtained a great victory over the forces of Chi, and ascribed the credit to the instructions of Confucius, whom Duke Kangtsu immediately invited to Lu. He went, but no proper post was available. He refused whatever offered, and retired to his private studies. He edited the Shu, transmitted the Li Ki, compiled the Odes, corrected the Music, and made a preface

for the Yi king.   He exhausted the Diagrams and improved
the written characters.   His disciples numbered 3000, of whom
seventy-two were proficients in all the Six Arts.   He had been
fourteen years absent from his native State.   The literary
work mentioned occupied five years.   His one original historical
work, the Chunchiw, was completed in 481, and in 479 he
died.   When the Chunchiw was finished, a *Lin* was caught
in the west of Lu.   This became a noted date.   His body was
buried in Weisze, north of the city of Lu.   There the whole of
his disciples mourned for him during the customary three
years.   But Tsu Kung remained for other three years, living
in a hut, when he too departed.   The son of Confucius died
before his father.   He had left a son Chi, named Tsuszu,
who compiled the Chungyung.

PERSECUTION.

Chin Shiwhang, after his family had been fighting for centuries, welded China into one kingdom in B.C. 221.   In 214
he built the Long Wall to protect his northern frontier against
the attacks of the fierce and restless Huns.

Next year he caused every particle of the writings which
treated of the Confucian method of government to be destroyed.   He believed, with a long line of predecessors, in
force, and had little faith in moral suasion.   Like most men
who do not believe in a higher form of spirituality, he was a
believer in magical methods, and hoped to obtain the pill of
immortality, the only immortal feature connected with which is
the search for it.   He died, succeeded by his son, who came to
a speedy end.   The Han dynasty took possession of the throne
in 206.   It was universally known that the late dynasty hated
the teachings of Confucius, and had, by its treatment of that
teaching, roused the detestation of the better class of Chinese,
and had therefore fallen in little more than a dozen years after
its establishment.   The new dynasty was wise enough to learn
the lesson.   Measures were taken to show their admiration
for Confucius.   The first emperor in B.C. 195 went to Lu,
where he offered the *Tailao*, or greatest sacrifice to Confucius.
Many old men could repeat whole passages from the forbidden
books.   Some books were restored in their entirety from
safe hiding-places.   The essentials of the doctrine in its original

setting were recovered. The name and influence of Confucius
were resuscitated. The second Emperor in 190 built Changan
as the capital, east of the river, on the west side of which was
the capital of Chin. For many years the Huns had been
powerful and aggressive, and so continued long after the Han
had cleared them out of Shensi. In A.D. 24 Changan was seized
and soon after retaken. It was seized a second time, and,
like the Chow in similar circumstances, the Han emperor, to
secure peace, removed the capital east to Loyang, which he
fortified in 25. A temple had to be erected there to his ancestors, and other business to be transacted which could not be
delayed. But in 29 the Emperor visited Lu, and sacrificed
at Tai Shan, which had been always associated with imperial
worship. On his return to Loyang, he went to inspect the
New College, which had just been completed. In 175, the
reigning emperor ordered the company of scholars to collate
the books then known and to correct the text. When the
work of revision was ended, they were commanded to engrave
the text of the Five Classics on stone slabs, that the corrected version might be handed down to future generations.
This was done in three different characters : (1) the Ancient
Style, which had been discovered in the wall which had been
broken down in the house of Confucius ; (2) the Seal Style
invented by Chin Shiwhang ; (3) the Square Style invented by
his Minister of Crime. For this purpose forty-six stone tablets
were engraved and set upright in front of the college in the
capital of Loyang. This immense labour was to ensure perfect
accuracy in the transmission of the Classics.

TITLES.

It may be of some interest to trace the manner in which
Confucius was regarded by successive generations of Chinese
rulers. In the fifth century B.C., Duke Ai of Lu styled him
Father Ni. In A.D. 1 the Han emperor styled him " Father Ni
the Universal." In 486 the title was " The Accomplished Sage
Father Ni." The Tang emperor in 637 styled him " Father Ni,
the Universal Sage." In 666 the Emperor, returning from
Tai Shan, worshipped Confucius at Chufu. In 733 his style
was " the Accomplished Universal Prince." In 905 Abaochi,
chief of the nomadic tribe of Kitan, in the south-west of
Manchuria, assumed the title of Whangti, rejecting the former

title of Kokhan, or Khan. The Emperor received his rank
from Heaven, and acknowledged the fact by offering special
sacrifices to Shangti. Abaochi consulted his ministers as to
the manner in which he should make his acknowledgments.
They recommended him to acknowledge Buddha as Supreme.
His heir objected that Buddha was not a Chinese religion,
that Kung Futsu was the great Sage honoured by ten thousand
generations. The Emperor was overjoyed, and ordered a
temple to be erected in honour of Confucius. It so happened
that a temple was then being built for Buddha, and another
for Taoism. The three were finished simultaneously. The
Emperor worshipped in that to Confucius, his Heir and the
Empress in the other two. In 952 the lord of the kingdom of
Chow went to Chufu to pay his respects at the temple of
Confucius within the city. When about to worship, his
minister attendants expostulated, saying that Confucius was
worthy to be a high official, but it was not right that the Son
of Heaven should worship him. He replied that Confucius
was the teacher of the emperors of a hundred generations,
and he dared not abstain from worshipping. He then worshipped, and repeated it a second time. A descendant of
Yen Yuen, the favourite disciple of Confucius, was resident
in the city. He was nominated a magistrate of the city and
Recorder. The Mongol emperor who was reigning in 1308
extended the title to the " Great Complete, Most Sage, Accomplished, Universal Prince." The Ming dynasty which followed
styled him the " Incomparable Teacher," inscribing on his
tablet the words, " Honoured of all, the Original and Perfect."
The tablet was afterwards called the " Divine Tablet of the
Most Sage, Incomparable, Learned, All-Pervading Confucius."
In 1645, next year after the occupation of Peking by the
Manchus, the title was the " Divine Seat of the Most Wise,
Incomparable Sage Confucius."

While honour to Confucius has been universal by all
the dynasties, and published to all men by the worship in
every city, the Chinese have never fallen into idolatry in
connection with this honour. The incongruity of an image of
Confucius or his disciples, with the spirit of their teaching,
may have preserved the country from the degradation connected with image worship. The Buddhist has fallen into this
incongruity. He has multiplied his images against the precept
and example of the founder. More strangely have Christians

dared to make an image to be worshipped of Him whose whole life consisted in proclaiming the spirituality of worship. The Confucianist deserves credit for consistently abstaining from making an image to be worshipped of their great teacher, though ascribing to him the attributes which properly are divine.

Though Chinese regard Confucius as the incomparable teacher, they have learned to place on an equality with him the Sage of the west, Jesus. They see that Europeans not only reverence Jesus as they reverence Confucius, but worship Him as the Son of God. Intelligent agnostics resent this superiority. The resentment is natural on the part of agnostics, who see no distinction between a Teacher and a Saviour. It was probably on this account that the late able Viceroy, Chang Chihtung, never rested till he persuaded the Empress Dowager to set Confucius on a spiritual pedestal on which he could be worshipped as a deity, and receive the honour of sacrifice by the Emperor when worshipping Heaven. There was no hint of an image. Now that the Revolution has swept away many superstitions, which had lingered in public life after all belief in them had died down, there can scarcely be retrogression. It is to be hoped that while the name of Confucius, as representing the best of Chinese thought, will be always held in reverence, the Chinese will avoid the stupidity of forming an image of him to be worshipped in any degree.

CHINESE ESTIMATE.

Though the Chinese mind differs from the western in its critical judgment, it is scarcely consistent with the highest judicial fitness to exclude the estimate by Chinese literary men of what is greatest and best in their own country, and for their own people. There has been in China no man whose teaching was so influential while the teacher was alive, and whose name after his death was so highly honoured and his influence so widespread as those of Confucius. Of his successors, none exceeds Mencius in clearness of penetration and depth of judgment.

He flourished two centuries after Confucius, and knew much about his disciples, through whom he had received the Confucian doctrines. His opinion of them was that they were men, all of whom would have attracted thoughtful minds to their court, yet not one was like their master. Three of them had seen and acknowledged the incomparable greatness of their teacher. But, able though they were and good, yet "from the beginning of mankind till now there has been none who can compare with Confucius." Speaking of ancient ministers, he mentioned two who were prominently distinguished, yet they had done some things which Mencius would not have copied. But his chief desire was to imitate Confucius in every detail of his life. Other sages were notable, some for one thing, some for another, but Confucius was like a "full pitched concert."

When Confucius was passing a certain country he was visited by an official who, after prolonged conversation, left saying to his disciples, "Why do you grieve that your Master is not in public office? The country has lost the Way, and Heaven is using Confucius to proclaim it, as the public crier makes proclamation by beat of drum."

At the death of Confucius, his disciples mourned for him throughout the full period. When they packed up their belongings to go home, Tsu Kung decided to remain in a hut for other three years. Bidding him farewell, the others wailed till they had no voice left. This betokened no ordinary teacher. Tsu Kung was himself no common man. Some compared him to Confucius, when he replied that he was like a five-foot wall, but Confucius was a wall of scores of feet, over which no one could see.

The books containing the principles of Confucius were very much alive for centuries after Mencius had passed away. Did those Classics contain merely incidents and sentiments transmitted from the past to satisfy the curiosity and meet the criticism of subsequent ages, the first Emperor of China would not have incurred the trouble, expense, and hostility involved in hunting and casting into the flames all the copies on which he could lay hands, and putting to death numbers of the best men in China who refused to surrender their books. The principles embedded in those books were opposed alike to his method of acquiring power and his methods of administration. They were his most dangerous enemies, whose influence would seriously prejudice his government. They were esteemed not as theory only, but as the practical rule of life and government. Therefore they had to be destroyed. Had the dynasty established by Chin Shi Whang honoured to a certain extent the moral principles of Confucianism, the dynasty could have survived a dozen years for every year of its actual existence.

The Confucian books were no sooner re-established than he was again set upon his pedestal. It may have been policy no less than admiration which induced the Han dynasty to adopt this attitude. It was a wise policy, and by it the dynasty continued to reign for centuries. To this day the Chinese people pride themselves on being the " children of Han." Since then his supremacy has been unquestioned. Succeeding ages made it more prominent. Since his time the Chinese have had great thinkers, men of exceptional talent, of critical minds, whose judgment no student can afford to ignore. All without exception agree in doing homage to him, the one man of China.

One reason which may partly account for depreciation of him is that he left no writing worthy of the name. His disciples pleaded with him to dictate to them in his own language the doctrines which he taught them orally. This he refused for some reason to do. The only original work of his is the " Spring and Autumn Annals," which has absolutely no style. It is as flat as a street of Caithness paving-stones. The age was an evil one. He put on record some public events concerning the State of Lu, covering a period of more than two centuries. The events recorded bore on the morality of government and were expressed in the briefest possible number of words. Yet this little volume is said to have made a great impression on the rulers of the period. The style of Mencius is good, and his mode of reasoning will compare with that of the philosophers of the west. The style of Szema Kuang in his voluminous history reminds one of the stately and voluptuous measure of Macaulay. But Chinese have never hesitated to place those as well as all other works on a plane beneath that of Confucius. Yet he wrote no treatise, elaborated no system, left no materials even to form an authoritative foundation for a philosophical work.

NO SPECULATION.

His work was that of editor. The principles of his editing are exemplified in what he omitted, perhaps even more suggestively than in what he has recorded. He has ruthlessly excluded, without apology, the loads of mythical story with which the ancient history of China introduces the beginnings of things. He does mention a few semi-mythical names, but each story has a moral for the rulers and the people of his time. It would be ungenerous to insinuate that he colours with his own ideas much of what he ascribes to the heroes of the olden time, but we must ascribe to him the design of recording, for the purpose of providing examples to be followed or beacons to be avoided, the incidents of the very early times with which his history begins. In the exclusion of the mythical we have a clue to his system of teaching. This clue is NO SPECULATION. He will have nothing but facts, and only such facts as speak out their clear message to men in their relationship as social beings. He disclaimed the rôle of keen visioned prophet who could penetrate the future. He would not soar on the wings of speculation to surprise or to dazzle his contemporaries. His character was that of the diligent and earnest student of the past to learn its lessons for the present. In his literary work he had one aim. That aim was UTILITY.

There is a school whose motto is " Art for Art's sake." Art is an end in itself, and has no business to inquire what the results are on the moral, mental, or physical condition of man. They forget that Art, when indifferent to morality, is unmoral, if not immoral, and that it terminates in the decadence of those influenced by it as in ancient Greece and "modern instances." Again, criticism for the sake of criticism degenerates into the display of cleverness. If in literature there be found writings whose tendency is to debase the moral nature of man, to emasculate his mind, to deprave his tastes, degrade his manners, or to brutalize his conduct, the overthrow of such literature is a boon to humanity. But in the case of a literature whose lessons are ennobling, whose ideals always urge men ever upward and onward in the way of liberty, of progress in all that tends to mental or physical improvement, the critic who exercises his skill or ingenuity to undermine the influence of it is guilty of injuring the human race just in proportion to his success in enfeebling the lessons and destroying the ideals. Literature cannot be neutral.

For what is the end of literature ? The answer sometimes is that literature is style, and applicable not to the matter, but to the manner of writing. Style in literature is like colour in Art. Colour is applied, according to Confucius, only after the ground is prepared. Colour in Art and style in

F

writing are of that sort of beauty which is said to be skin deep.
Beneath the skin is the substantial body in accordance with
whose lines and nature beauty is more or less lasting. Literary
form is important only in proportion to the value of the substance enclosed in the form. The noblest effect of literature
is not to amuse, but to instruct ; the former is a passing
cloud, the latter a fertilising shower. Confucius was particular as to the language he employed, for the "skin of a
tiger or leopard divested of its hair is like the skin of a sheep
or a dog with its hair off." Good literature provides one of
the great pleasures of life, but the real purpose of literature
is the improvement of mankind. The more agreeable its form
the better it is adapted to its purpose. Confucius believed
the best form to be that which sets forth most clearly and
unmistakably the meaning of the writer. His own editorial
work was to record the thought and action of the past for the
use of the present and the future. It was not in order to em-
balm the memory of the dead, but by the lessons from the
dead to exhort the living. The past can be seen in a completed form ; we see the beginning, the course, and the ending
of action as we cannot see it in contemporary events. From
history we are able to infer how a given course of action is
likely to terminate. Conduct of a similar character is likely
to produce similar results. This is the key to the attitude of
Confucius on literature. He was as insistent on studying the
best in the literature of the past in order to attain the highest
possible development of human nature, as the most ardent
apostle of culture in our own day. On the necessity for politeness he was more emphatic than modern culture-worshippers.
In this respect his words and example have exerted a potent
influence upon the literary men of China from his time to the
present. There more perhaps than in other lands has culture
been made the standard of life. In no other country can the
influence of culture apart from living religion be more ad-
vantageously studied, for there it has produced the best that
man can attain by his own innate and independent powers.
The culture of the west has borrowed its altruism, its morality,
and most of its vital teaching from Christianity. When
examined apart from the prejudices common to all uncultured
people coming in contact with a civilisation different from
their own, culture has no reason to be ashamed of its fruits

in China. Independently of Christianity, no system of philosophy can anywhere show results comparable to what culture
has done for China. The lessons of her great teacher of culture
demand therefore a sympathetic hearing from the cultured
folk of other lands. The man of culture will be the first to discover by the careful study of those teachings the reason why
Confucius is to this day regarded as the incomparable teacher
by all the learned of the most populous kingdom in the world.

SUBJECTS OF LECTURE.

If he wrote no treatise on the subjects on which he taught,
his speech enforcing and explaining them was endless. His
method of instruction was lecturing. On some matters he
refused to lecture. These were four :—(1) The Strange ; (2)
Physical Force; (3) Disorder or Anarchy; (4) The Spirit World.
On five subjects his speech was endless :—(1) Humaneness ;
(2) Integrity ; (3) Propriety ; (4) Knowledge ; (5) Truth.
In connection with (3) were the duties inherent in the Five
Relations :—(1) Sovereign and Minister ; (2) Father and Son ;
(3) Husband and Wife ; (4) Elder and Younger Brother ; (5)
Friends. The systematic collection of his teaching was not
his work ; it was done long after his time by disciples who
had heard the discourses. These groups of words were,
however, the texts on which was based the teaching of his
life. No connected discourse exists on any of these subjects.
What remains is but an infinitesimal portion of what he taught.
It consists of terse, epigrammatic, or antithetic gems in isolation, phrases or sentences wrenched out of their context and
embalmed in the memory by their own intrinsic force, beauty,
or novelty. The phrases retained were not only memorable,
but clearly understood from the circumstances in which they
were uttered. One of his ablest disciples has recorded that
his numerous discourses on Human Nature and the Decree of
Heaven were beyond the comprehension of the hearers. These
are completely lost, except a few fragments made prominent
by the circumstances in which they were spoken. This acknow-
ledgment of ignorance indicates, however, that he was not
so reticent on the subject of Religion as he is sometimes represented.

That his lectures and expositions were of an exceptional

character is evidenced by the impression produced on his contemporaries. His disciples adored him. Kings and princes honoured him while he was alive and worshipped him after his death, even when they did not accept him as guide. Every succeeding age of scholars has acknowledged the unique character of the man. Discarding speculation, and disclaiming the name, or fame of novelty in philosophy or political principles, he had one aim in life. He dug deep in the annals of the forgotten past and unfolded principles of ethics and politics most surely believed by the great and good whose names were the heritage of the Chinese people. The principles were not novel, as the human relations were not new; but the phraseology employed and the illustrations used to explain and enforce them were new, or they would not have been so impressive.

Thus have we traced four elements characteristic of his teaching :—(1) his remarkable knowledge of antiquity, from the time of the Hia dynasty; (2) his familiarity with all details of Ceremonial bearing upon Propriety; (3) his uncompromising integrity; (4) the keenness of his intellect in revealing the fundamentals of ethics and politics, and his ability to apply them practically for the wellbeing of all classes of the community, privately and socially, in the establishment and administration of laws, in the exposition and proper discharge of the relative duties. For all forms of duty he found a basis in REVERENCE. He was notably free from the superstitions of his time and country. He was said to be without prejudices, foregone conclusions, obstinacy and egoism, willing and able to learn from the most humble individuals. He did not claim the superhuman abilities and excellences which his countrymen have ascribed to him. He did not pretend to have intuitive knowledge of his doctrines. On the contrary, he claims to have derived them from hard study. He was not a Sage nor a man of Humaneness, though he strove without weariness to attain that character. He did claim to be the equal of any man in literature, but did not presume to be a "noble" man, able to embody his knowledge fully in his life. He regretted his inability to do always what was virtuous, to follow the right and correct the wrong. He could not serve in perfection dukes and high officials in public, nor his father and elder brother at home. He was unable to exert his utmost in mourning, to treasure up knowledge in silence, to learn without fatigue, or to instruct without weariness.

To Music he attached great importance. The Odes arouse the mind, Propriety makes it steadfast, but Music completes character. When in the kingdom of Chi he heard the music called Shao. Its perfection was such that for the following three months he was unable to eat meat. The music called Kwanswi was joyous but not licentious, mournful without excessive grief. He disliked the light music of Ching. Good government should cultivate the Shao, and banish the Ching, along with glib-tongued men. The songs of Ching were licentious, and glib-tongued men dangerous. After his return from Wei he paid considerable attention to the music of Court and people, editing and amending both.

CHAPTER III.

CONFUCIUS, RELIGION.

So great was the importance attached by Confucius to Ceremonialism as emblematic of and conducive to order in public government and in private life, that some students suppose him to have been agnostic on all religious subjects. The scanty references to Religion in his recorded teaching lend some authority to this inference. On the other hand are students who make his system one of Three Religions accepted by Chinese. This opinion is based on an erroneous translation. The word translated " Religion " should be translated " Instruction." The system to the teaching of which he devoted his life is purely Politico-ethical. To discover his attitude towards Religion one has to dig beneath the surface, but it is a matter which demands and repays thorough research.

Among the great teachers of mankind, Confucius seems to me to stand in a category by himself. In Greece, in India, in Arabia, philosophic teachers reasoned on ethics and politics, but in their practical teaching there was in every instance a mixture of unsubstantial speculation on matters invisible. Confucius, on the contrary, rejected everything savouring of speculation. Scraps from his teaching on all subjects were eagerly treasured by his disciples. But they never caught him tripping, even informally, in the ways of opinions which he could not substantiate. " No speculation " is the principle underlying every one of his expressed sentiments. Yet a thinker so powerful, of such untiring diligence, must have had his times of indulging in speculation, especially as his mind was essentially analytic and inquisitive. But these speculations he kept strictly locked away in the darkest corners of his mind. One aphorism of his bears on this characteristic. It is, closely translated, " to know that you know, and to know that you do not know, that is knowledge." This conception of knowledge excludes everything unsupported by indisputable fact, or incontrovertible reasons. Mere guess work, or theories based on mental clouds, he disdainfully ignored. This principle of " no speculation " is exemplified in and explanatory of the *Lunyu*, or " Selections." If the principle is understood it becomes a key to open the door into his mind on Religion.

He was free from preconceived prejudices. From the time when he began to learn with intelligence to the end of his life he was continually bent on the acquisition of knowledge, and believed it no disgrace to ask for information from all sorts and conditions of men, though they might be his inferiors intellectually and by education. When the subject under investigation became clear beyond the possibility of question, he knew that he knew it, and felt thenceforth free to teach it.

In the remarkable passage in which he informed his disciples of his gradual growth in learning, experience, and knowledge, he said that the love of study took possession of him in his fifteenth year. Then he began to learn the characters in which were entombed the great past of his forefathers. He began to meditate and inquire, making the acquisition of knowledge the one overmastering aim of his life. He began to use his eyes with discrimination. At first he believed every man's word. As he grew older he became more inquisitive, critical, and sceptical. He learned to look for conduct corresponding to words. He noticed human life around, with all its complexities, its wants and their gratification. He meditated on what he read and on what he saw in social life. He observed the wonderful variety combined with harmony of living beings on earth. He saw the goodness and wickedness of human life, with its mixture of happiness and misery. At thirty the amount of his digested knowledge was such that on many subjects he had no mental hesitancy. But instead of resting satisfied, he was the more eager to make further inroads on the domain of those subjects which he knew he did not know. His thirst for knowledge was no less, but he had come to learn that action was at least as important as accurate knowledge, or the investigation which secured it. From that time he endeavoured to guide his life in accord-

ance with the knowledge which he had acquired. He resolved to embody in practice what he had concluded was
right. Such was his progress that at forty he was free from
doubt or hesitancy. He saw truths not as isolated fragments,
but as separate entities connected by underlying principles,
which tended to unify them. At length all his perplexities
came to an end. At fifty he came to the definite conclusion
that all happens by the Decree of Heaven. He discovered
that behind the apparent diversities and contradictions in
human affairs, in terrestrial and celestial phenomena, there
was, invisible to the thoughtless, a Divine purpose, silently,
unostentatiously but surely, rough hewing all events to one
intelligent and righteous end. He recognised that all beings
and all affairs are completely under the control of Almighty
and All-knowing Heaven. No event happens by chance.
Nothing great or small occurs without the directing will and
control of Heaven. This outcome of his studious life brought
him into line with the basis of the Original Religion of China,
'viz., that everything depended on the Decree of Heaven.

When passing through the State of Wei, the Duke sought
his advice on the Art of war, which was then chronic between
the States. He replied that from his youth he had applied
himself to study the meaning of the sacrificial vessels, and had
not studied the Art of war, on which he could not, therefore,
express any opinion. He refused to give positive answers to
questions on the abnormal, on force, on anarchy, and on the
spirit world. He spoke of the common, not the abnormal;
of virtue, not of force ; of orderly government, not of anarchy ;
of man, not of the spirit world. To the question how one
could best serve the spirits of the dead, he replied, "If you
fail completely to fulfil your duties to the living, how can
you serve the spirits ? " These instances suffice to illustrate
his principle of "no speculation." The subject must be
cloudlessly clear in his mind before he was satisfied that he
knew and could teach it. The movements, imaginings, and
questions, unsubstantial, incapable of logical demonstration,
or lacking the evidence of facts in the underground depths of
his mind, he would voice not even to his favourite pupil or to
his son. This principle is adequate explanation of much
that was enigmatical or seemingly unreasonable in his refusal
to reply to some grave questions.

Of these the most important were about the condition of man after death, and of the spirits, whether of ancestors or of heroes, worshipped by the people. The Odes were largely composed of descriptions of sacrifices offered to these. They entered fully into the life of the people. He was familiar with the beliefs and practices of the ancients in connection with them. The book of Odes was his favourite study. The few statements made by him regarding the spirits prove that he had thought deeply on the subject. The Odes teach that the spirits of ancestors exist, that they come and go, that they are now in Heaven, anon on earth, now present and again absent. But though the views and practices of the ancients are to him sacred, he had failed to attain full conviction of the actual existence of spirits, and of their presence among men. He therefore refused to answer questions regarding the spirit world. He would not publish opinions for dogmas, nor unsettle the minds of others by the doubtings of his own. His teaching was uncompromisingly utilitarian. He continued, however, the ancient custom of pouring out a libation to the spirits when about to partake of food, and to offer the sacrifices handed down from ancestors, though he professed ignorance of their significance. This homage to ancient custom was no evidence of belief. He did not object to serve the spirits by sacrifice, provided such offerings did not interfere with the routine of the duties of normal life. The mutual relations of man to man were always with us, and always insistent on attention. If spirits did take an intelligent interest in the doings of their descendants, they could not be displeased with those descendants if, while not neglecting the customary offerings, they were careful to discharge the duties devolving on them towards the living. His principles and practice would oppose such customs as exist in the Greek and Roman Catholic Churches connected with the numerous saints' days which claim so many days of idleness in the year.

But, though deprecating as unwise much mental distraction, devotion of time or sacrifice of means in service to the unseen spirits, he demanded the retention of the ancient ceremonial and devout sincerity in whatever services were rendered. The ruler of a State offered officially a sheep at the tomb of his ancestors on the first day of the twelfth moon. Confucius in his teaching did not give as much prominence as the ancients to the service of the spirits ; his disciples may therefore have concluded that he considered it a matter of minor importance. One of them expressed the opinion that the offering of a sheep was a useless waste. Confucius rebuked him, because he made the sheep of more consequence than the ceremonial.

But no man had any business to offer sacrifices to the ancestors of other people in the hope of obtaining extra benefits. This was a work of officious supererogation. More serious still was the offence of him who offered sacrifice to the spirits of the ancestors of men of higher rank than himself. Contrary to this rule, an official, Li, had offered sacrifice to the god of the mountain, Tai Shan. This sacrifice was the special prerogative of the emperor, or of the ruler of Lu. Confucius denounced the crime as so serious that the offender could find no place for prayer, for he had offended against the Decree of Heaven, which had bestowed on emperor and duke their rank and office.

In every sacrifice rendered to the spirits, Sincerity was indispensable. Though not without some appearance of inconsistency between some of his own conduct and his teaching, he insisted that sincerity was an essential element, leavening the whole of a good man's life. One without sincerity was useless as a cart without a yoke. So much importance did he attach to it, that he declared the sacrifice to be no sacrifice if offered by deputy when the descendant of the object of worship was able to discharge the duty himself. He also demanded that whatever the belief of the worshipper, his offering must be made as devoutly, and the ceremonial observed as completely, as though he knew for a certainty that the spirits were present. In all this there was a mental hesitancy so decided that we can quite understand why, acting on his fundamental principle, he declined to answer questions of mere curiosity concerning the spirits of the unseen world. The same process of reasoning explains his reticence on theories regarding death.

That he avoided all dubiety and speculation in his oral teaching is further attested by the nature of the subjects which he commonly and emphatically did teach. These are mentioned as a series of subjects on which the "noble" man thinks cautiously and acts with deliberation. There are nine subjects which claim his whole-hearted attention :—(1) he seeks clearness of vision in what he sees ; (2) to understand what he hears ; (3) to be gentle in manner ; (4) to regard others with respect ; (5) to be truthful in speech ; (6) to be reverent in serving ; (7) to think of difficulties when angry ; (8) to investigate when in doubt ; (9) to think of righteousness when gain presents itself. These subjects are so universal in their application that every man is everywhere and always affected by them. On these he had meditated so that he knew that he knew them. They were the subjects of his ordinary teaching.

HEAVEN.

But the reasoning which explains his refusal to discuss ancestral spirits and death does not apply to what seems to be his intentional neglect of dogmatic instruction on the Decree of Heaven and on Religion. The statements quoted below show how full-hearted was his faith in the relation of man to, and his dependence upon, the invisible over-ruling Power called Heaven. For the guidance of his own private life he accepted in its entirety the dogmatism of the Original Religion of China concerning Heaven and the Decree of Heaven. The careful study of these statements leads to the conclusion that it was no mental hesitancy which caused him to abstain from dogmatic teaching regarding the All Ruler.

When Confucius visited the State of Wei, he was invited to interview the wife of the duke who was reputed to be living a disorderly life. He accepted the invitation. One of his disciples blamed him because it was improper for him to visit such a woman. To him the visit seemed probably one purely of ceremony. He replied that if his visit had been contrary to the principles of propriety, and in contravention of the Way, Heaven would forsake him. This statement justifies the supposition of a commentator that he may have had some hopes of winning the woman to a better life, for why if unwilling to change should she have sent for him whose character and opinions were universally known. To us the incident is

valuable as an indication of his belief in the continuous wit-
nessing presence of the Supreme, and in His intelligent and
just reward of every act.

On one occasion, when he was unwell and supposed to be
dying, one disciple nominated another to be an official, so that
should their master die, his obsequies would be those of a
high official. On recovering he rebuked his too zealous
disciples, asking how they had dared to lie in treating him
who was no great official as though he were one. Whom did
they attempt to deceive by their action? Could they cheat
Heaven? Heaven knew all things, and man in all things
should be true. To an exclamation of his that no man knew
him, one responded, "What, not know Confucius?" He
replied that he understood the affairs of men below and in-
vestigated the principles of Heaven above. In all this no man
understood him, but, he added emphatically, "Heaven under-
stands me." He did not always succeed in getting his own
way, which he believed to be the right way, yet he did not
murmur against Heaven, who had thwarted him, nor blame
men when they differed from and opposed him. This,
however, was no cause of grief to him, because Heaven
knew him.

The noble man entertains fear regarding three things.
He fears the Decree, the Law, and the Sayings of the Sage.
The fear of the Decree was not an empty dread. It is the fear
of trespassing in any way against the will of Heaven, or of
neglecting to meet its claims. If he oppose or fail to observe
it, he turns his back on Heaven, and Heaven will cast him off.
His fear makes wilful disobedience impossible, and acts as a
stimulus to exert his utmost in observing the principles which
are binding always and everywhere. But it is the noble man
who is influenced by this fear. The "mean" man may know
about the Decree and the principles, but he will not fear it
nor observe them.

A disciple was lamenting the fact that while all the others
had brothers, he had none. His fellow-disciples checked him,
saying, "Don't you remember the master saying that 'Birth
and death are by Decree, wealth and honour are the gifts of
Heaven?'" If birth is by Decree, it follows that the Decree
precedes the birth, and if decreed the birth cannot but follow.

If not decreed, there can be no birth. Knowing this, the noble man will honour and submit to the will of Heaven and refrain from murmuring. If birth and death are by Decree as well as all the conditions between these extremes, the noble man shall guide his life according to this belief. His conduct will be always reverent. He will be respectful to man, and act consistently with the dictates of propriety. Then shall all men within the limits of the four seas be his brethren. He can have no reason to grieve that he has no brothers.

Whan Tui, chief minister of the State of Sung, plotted to kill Confucius when he was teaching his disciples under the shade of a tree. Because of that hostility, the disciples urged him to flee. He replied, " This talent was given to me by Heaven, what then can Whan Tui do to me ? " Heaven having imposed upon him a duty which was intended for the well-being of mankind, would not fail him while he was in the way of discharging it. If Heaven did not wish to destroy it, what foe could injure him ? This was his way of saying that he was immortal till his work was done. A belief such as this is conducive to peace of heart, says a commentator, but does not nullify the duty of exerting oneself to avoid danger.

On the death of Yen Yuen, his favourite disciple, he cried out in deepest grief, " Heaven destroys me ! Heaven destroys me ! " This disciple could from a few words deduce a principle. When he understood any practical truth he applied it with all diligence to his daily life. In learning, in natural abilities, and in the practical application of his knowledge, he was superior to his fellow-disciples. Confucius anticipated that after his own death Yuen would carry on his work. He was not anxious about the death of his body, but was deeply concerned about the transmission of his doctrine, which made for the well-being of humanity. Now that Heaven had called away his young disciple, he became hopeless about the future of that doctrine, and in anguish of soul cried out that Heaven was destroying him.

An official in the State of Kwang was hated on account of his oppression of the people. When Confucius was travelling in the neighbourhood of that State, he was taken for that official, to whom he bore a remarkable resemblance. A band

of men surrounded him for five days, threatening to take his
life. He encouraged his terrified disciples, saying that the
learning which embodied the true doctrine was once entrusted
to King Wen and Duke Chow. By Decree of Heaven it was
now in his possession. If Heaven had desired the destruction of the doctrine why was he put in charge of it ? If Heaven
desired the survival of that doctrine the men who were clam-
ouring against him could do no harm.

At another court a minister, Bai Liao, was persecuting the
doctrine. A follower angrily threatened to denounce the
persecutor in the public market and the magisterial court.
Confucius said, " If the doctrine is to succeed, its success
will be owing to the Decree ; if it is to perish, its fate will
depend on the Decree. With this Decree what has Bai Liao
to do ? " His belief implied that even if the persecution
should banish the doctrine from court, the success of the
persecution would have been already decided by the Decree
of Heaven.

His disciples were anxious to retain in writing an accurate
representation of his doctrine, and requested him to dictate
to them the exact verbiage which would most accurately embody the truth for permanent use. He objected, and to an
exclamation of surprise said, " Heaven does not speak."
They were allowed to ponder over the answer, and to discover
that without verbal utterance the principles of Heaven were
patent to every earnest thinker. The seasons revolve in
order, all sorts of beings are born, each at its own time and
its due season. Heaven speaks not, but is revealed by the
heavens above and the earth beneath, by the wonderful rule
of law in the infinite variety and fundamental harmony of
the working of nature.

One statement of his has been a perennial puzzle to the
materialistic commentators from the tenth century down.
Once when very seriously unwell a disciple asked his per-
mission to go in his name to pray for recovery by offering
sacrifices to the spirits of heaven and earth. He replied,
" My praying has been of old." Commentators have explained that his prayer consisted of a blameless life, which
required no prayer to deprecate the wrath, nor sacrifice to
secure the goodwill of, the spirits. Such an exposition could

be satisfactory only to men ready to silence difficult questions by a little bit of self-deception. What the significance was of his " praying of old " is less enigmatical to those who examine it in the light of the preceding sentences, which show his faith to be undoubting in an all-powerful, ever-present, all-ruling Providence. His trust in the interference on his behalf of that same Providence is clearly evident. His praying was of a kind unknown to and unseen by his disciples. Prayer by the means of offerings through the medium of ritual was to him no prayer at all. His praying had been unseen of men because it was in sincerity of heart before Him who, without the medium of words, reads the desires of the heart.

It seems clear from the preceding statements that he entertained no shadow of doubt in the ceaseless and benefi-cent activity of the Power that makes for Righteousness. He was a convinced believer who trusted in God with devoted reverence and unquestioning confidence in times of danger as of peace. With this unmistakable evidence of the re-ligious character of Confucius, the question will still more urgently press itself upon us, Why did he abstain from teaching religious dogma to his disciples ?

There are two ways of answering this question. The first is based on the fundamental principle of his teaching. The Being and the character of God are not known in the same sense as mathematical subjects are known. They cannot be proved as it can be that two and two make four. The evi-dence is circumstantial. It is based on probability. Hence, though his mind was free from doubt, his reason could not avoid some degree of that speculation which he had so com-pletely rejected. To myself this is explanation sufficient.

But there is another more likely reason. It is traceable not to him, but to his disciples. In the Four books we have the memorabilia preserved because of some peculiarity. On certain subjects he refused to speak. They were strange phenomena, deeds of mere strength, rebellious disorder, and supernatural beings, whether subordinate deities or spirits of the departed ancestors. It is recorded that he lectured commonly on the Odes, History, Propriety, and Ceremonial, of which lec-tures the merest scraps remain from the teaching of a couple of score years. He lectured much on general literature and culture, which the disciples understood. But they declare that many lectures on Human Nature and the Decree of Heaven they did not understand. This chink lets us into the secret. Numerous lectures spread over many years are completely lost because they were not understood. The disciples could condense into crisp sentences what they understood. The deeper subjects which they did not understand could not be thus treated, and he refused their request to dictate the very words which would express his teaching on Human Nature and the Decree. Hence these great subjects are represented by a few references which were made intelligible by the circumstances in which they were uttered. If, then, so little exists of his teaching about the Supreme Ruler, it is simply because the disciples failed to understand his speech. Did some of that unrecorded lore not pass down to Mencius, who treated so fully and so clearly of human nature ? We must also take into account, what is usually ignored, that Confucius was responsible for the verbiage of the *Shu*, which, for a period of over a thousand years, reveals the purest monotheism (see " Original Religion of China "). Consistently with the reverence which forbade him to name his sovereign, he invariably uses the name Heaven instead of the personal name Supreme Ruler. Throughout Chinese history the two are synonymous.

Carelessness alone can claim Confucius as an agnostic. It was no fault of his that the philosophers of the Sung dynasty adopted agnosticism, to do which they had to misinterpret the passages on the Decree of Heaven which stared at them from out the Classics.

Confucius was not puzzled with the problem of Job. He accepted life as it appeared. The bad man suffers and suffers justly. The good man also suffers, but he will not say, like Job, that he suffers unjustly. He leaves the unravelling of the knot with God who is essentially good. There, too, Job had ultimately to leave it.

Confucius and his disciples were travelling once when they fell short of food. The disciples expressed surprise that a good man should be allowed to suffer want. He replied that a good man may suffer want, but if a mean man suffered want he would become lawless. The bad man rebels, the good man submits to the will of Heaven. In judging him, we must remember that Confucius is not only imperfectly reported, but that he lived in the sixth century B.C., and possessed the illumination only which came from the founders of the Chow dynasty six centuries before his time.

Collating the sentences commented on above, with much cognate matter which has to be omitted in this book, we may summarise the creed revealed by them as follows :— God, or Heaven, is the Creator, personal, intelligent, all-wise, just, good, long-suffering, ceaselessly caring for His creatures, interfering to protect them from enemies however powerful, witness of all events in the deepest darkness as at noonday. In all this he was a man of faith, and because of all this he was a man of prayer. His creed concerning himself was that God made him, endowed him with certain qualities of mind and body, bestowed upon him a nature which was essentially good, for God being good could give him no other. God was always with him, and would, while his life was of use to his fellow-men, protect him from serious danger. His duty and desire, therefore, were while he had a being to use the mind and the body which God had given him with all their endowments to carry out God's will among men. He believed that will to be the moral and physical improvement of mankind. His duty could be discharged by imparting to men the principles the knowledge of which he had acquired. When his task was completed God would, at His own time, call him hence, where and when he could not discover, but left unhesitatingly with the Supreme Ruler. We cannot refrain from thinking that this noble soul, so richly endowed, with so exalted an estimate of truth and duty, must have often pondered over the passage in his favourite Odes : " King Wen is above in the immediate presence of God."

But in the world on which had fallen moral and intellectual blindness, and was guided by a spirit of materialism and brute force, his religion was a matter between his secret heart and God. It was manifested in the unceasing desire to regulate his life so as to gain the goodwill of the Just One, who was good and would tolerate no evil. His faith was shown not in creed and ritual, but in the words and works of his daily life. Out of thick darkness he appeared a comet, and the pale light emitted by him has come down even to our time. Compared

G

with his contemporaries in Canaan, may we not conclude that he was one of those who " in every nation fearing God and working righteousness are accepted of Him " ? Here we have a man and a system so closely related to Christianity that the missionary will find in them the most powerful leverage with which to raise the Chinese people into the blazing light of the fullness of knowledge of God as the Father of mercies, whose love is over all His works and underlies and embraces all His character.

CHAPTER IV

EARLY BOOKS.

Books are inseparably connected with letters. Of the number of books in China and the subjects of them there is no end. Here it is intended only to give the Chinese account of the utility of books, and of the rise of, and reason for, some of the classics which have been the study and the guide of China, and reveal the secret of her civilisation and long persistence.

When the illiterate Manchus entered Peking as conquerors in 1644, they invited a company of eminent Chinese scholars to join them in providing a Manchu translation of the principal Chinese classics. To accompany this translation they issued a " Complete Commentary " in 1735, for which they drew up a good historical and explanatory preface. In it they state that in the early days there were no errors. Truth was was clear as the sun in a cloudless sky, so that books on ethical subjects were not required. In the decadence of the Chow dynasty learning was neglected, instruction despised, manners and customs degraded. Then appeared Confucius, who made it his life-work to unfold truth and to combat error. As no ruler was at once wise and good enough to patronise him, he was obliged to depend on his own unaided scholarship and energy. By oral teaching and by editing of the good literature of the past on law, customs. and ceremonial, he provided a guide for all future ages. Nevertheless, though he had taught three thousand students, his doctrines were, after his death, in danger of falling into oblivion. One of his disciples compiled a treatise founded on his lectures, which he called the " Great Learning," or learning for men. This disciple was the teacher of the grandson of Confucius, in whose time errors were so boldly proclaimed that the voice of truth could not be heard. To counteract this evil he issued a book, also based on the teaching of Confucius, which he called "Chung Yung," or the "Invariable Middle," the sole object of which was to proclaim truth. His doctrines were caught up and widely proclaimed by Mencius, after whose time the river of truth began again to become muddy. Truth was all but annihilated, agriculture was ruined, disturbance was universal; there was no prospect of escape from national destruction. But in the cycle of heaven there is no departure from which there is no subsequent return. With the establishment of the Sung dynasty learning revived, and rule and order were restored. The two brothers Cheng appeared, the work of Mencius was revived, and again became influential. The teaching of the ancient worthies shone again resplendent in the world.

Chutsu was a disciple of the brothers, and flourished in 1186. He introduced the "Small Learning," or learning for little people. He mentions that in olden times the sons of king, baron, and all high officials went to the Junior School at eight years of age. They were instructed how to sprinkle and to brush the room, the hall, and the schoolroom, to respond and reply to parents, or their superiors in rank or in age, and to advance and retire when receiving or escorting guests. They were introduced to ceremonial, of which there were twelve varieties connected with sacrifices on felicitous and five for sad occasions; there were five forms of ceremony in the army and six at feasting. They were taught music, of which there were six kinds; archery, of which there were five varieties; and charioteering (driving a chariot of four horses), of which there were five different ways. They began reading books, which were in six varieties of characters, and reckoning, of which there were nine kinds. At fifteen the youth assumed the cap of manhood, and entered the High School, where he was set to study the "Great Learning." The time spent in the junior school devoted to the Small Learning was supposed to have opened his mind to think.

In his preface to the Small Learning, Chutsu says that though the book was destroyed by Chin Shi Whang, fragments were found in other books which indicated that the contents did not vary in their teaching from those of the other classics.

Its opening sentence stated its object to be to show that the "origin, permanence, prosperity, perfection of all beings are the design and care of the constant Way of Heaven, the self-originated and invariable Substance." The instruction received from the Small Learning re-establishes the heart, and nourishes the virtuous disposition as the root of the tree is strengthened. The Great Learning opens and expands the understanding, so that the scholar lives in virtue and increases in merit as a tree extends its branches.

THE GREAT LEARNING.

This book is a treatise based on recollections of the teachings of Confucius. Its first sentence gives its text. This is to "make known illustrious virtue, to renovate the people, and to stop only when it has attained the highest perfection." The underlying principle of its teaching is that this end is to be attained, not by the institution of new laws, nor by changes in the customs of the people, nor by the application of force, but by the proper regulation of one's own conduct. When the life of the ruler is in perfect harmony with the right, his family shall follow his example, their influence again shall extend to their neighbours, and thus the leavening process shall gradually extend to the remotest parts of the empire. The contents of the book are clustered around four catch-words : (1) Humaneness or Benevolence, which is defined as gentleness, harmony, pity, mercy, and love ; (2) Integrity or Righteousness, defined as judging, governing, deciding in strict accordance to rule ; (3) Ceremonial or Propriety, defined as the expression of reverence and honour ; (4) Knowledge or Widsom, defined as the differentiation of right and wrong. These embrace the entire ethical nature of man, and imply his complete duty. Subsequently, when the number five became fashionable, a fifth catch-word was added—Truth or Sincerity. The book may be considered as an ethico-philosophical-treatise on government. It is one of the most logically-constructed of the classics.

CHUNG-YUNG, or EQUILIBRIUM.

In medio tutissimus. The Roman thought of safety. The Chinese term is to a casual glance open to the same explanation.

This is, however, a misunderstanding of which no student of Chinese should be guilty. The literal translation of the two words is " middle-constant." But they refer only to moral conduct. The way of morality is a narrow and straight path, on each side of which is a ditch of dangerous error. Going in that path there must be no turning to right or left hand, the way is straight on. It is the way of equilibrium between two opposite errors. The kernel of the book is that the " Decree of Heaven created the disposition or nature of man. The Way is that which ' leads out ' or trains this nature. Instruction is the method of keeping this way in repair." The book is a collection of the sententious phrases of Confucius, forming a dissertation, theoretical and practical, on his ethical system. The grandson of Confucius strung these together in a systematic treatise, such as Confucius himself declined to emit. It forms one of the best books existing in any language for the instruction of the young scholar in ethics.

LUN YU, OR SELECTIONS.

This book is more characteristic of the teachings of Confucius than any other. It was compiled by two disciples, and is composed of *disjecta membra*, phrases pithy, epigrammatic, independent, full flavoured of the Confucian mind and manner. No translation can give a perfect rendering of it. In the course of his many years' instruction, whether in formal lectures or more familiar conversation, many thousands of such aphorisms would have dropped from his lips which are for ever lost. Those which have survived are such as by striking phraseology or notable application made an indelible impression on his disciples.

These books cannot be said to give an adequate representation of the lessons imparted throughout his long life by the great teacher. They provide no classification of his ethics, nor do they attempt a systematic treatment of his teaching. Careful examination leads to the inference that we have in them but the bare statement of the themes on which he lectured, or memorable phrases noted down from his discourses. The verbiage from the themes and phrases is probably his own. There is no example of the manner in which they were discussed, nor of the reasoning by which they were illustrated and enforced. They show us what he taught, but not how he taught. Though they do not indicate to us his methods, we are not to conclude that in his mind he had no method. The one overmastering design of his life was to raise good rulers of good citizens. The art of good government handed down the ages was the basis of his teaching. From this centre radiated all the ethical qualities needful to make man virtuous citizens of a peaceful nation. Not, therefore, the mutual relationship of the virtues was his theme, but their particular influence on his thesis. Though he had sympathetic hearers, he had no elucidating Plato. The virtues regarded by him as necessary to man are recorded by his disciples in the Lun Yu in jerky sentences and a fragmentary manner. Yet by comparing the fragments we are able to form a fair conception of the relationship between, and the relative importance of, the more fundamental virtues. The conclusion is that in Christianity alone do we find a system of ethics unquestionably higher than his. Between the two there is a remarkable affinity. The word we translate " humaneness " bears the meaning and exerts the influence we ascribe to the Christian " charity." As love is the perfection of the law, so out of the root of humaneness grow up all moral excellences.

These books of Confucius, with the Odes and History which preceded them, and the books of Mencius which followed them, have taxed and trained the minds of the generations since their time, and are all implied in what is called Confucianism.

CHAPTER V.

The Sage.

The Sage stands above all other men, of whatever rank or condition. The character which represents him in literature expresses pictorially his relation to mankind. An "ear" and a "mouth" stand over a "king." The king can pour out his difficulties into the ear of the sage, who can unravel them. He inculcates his duty or reprimands his errors. He is super-eminent in natural endowments and in acquired knowledge. Knowledge in the sage attains its highest development, and is manifested in a life exercising the greatest possible influence for good. Sages were the originators in all improvements in social life, discovered new truths, or made new applications of known truth. From the very earliest period they were the agents in raising mankind in the various stages of an ascending civilisation. One may be master of all the knowledge embedded in the literature of the past, and be able to explain all the difficulties which occur to the mind of man, but if his life be not one of practical goodness, he is not a sage. He may issue from the privacy of his study his views and speculations about man. But however wise, these do not constitute him a sage. Not because of what is in him is he a sage, but because of what he can do for the benefit of mankind. He is essentially a man of affairs. He guides rightly not his own life only, but the life of others. When his deeds correspond to his words, and his words to his deeds, and these are of the highest and best, presenting an example guiding men into goodness and comfort, then is he entitled to the name of sage. The sages of the past in China are those whose wisdom, knowledge, talents, and active goodness were such as to make them men head and shoulders above all others. They became rulers over the empire because they were best qualified to guide men in the way they should go, to protect the good and to punish the evil, to procure general peace and to provide universal content.

In the political confusion existing for centuries before and after Confucius, the principles of the ancient rulers insisting on peace might receive a respectful hearing, but they had no influence over court or camp. Men who had been officials and ministers resigned their posts because they could hold them only in endless conflict with their principles. They retired to remote villages and sequestered valleys, where the intrigues of courts and the clashing of arms would not disturb their souls or harass their feelings. They betook themselves to agriculture and affected the life of the recluse, if not of the ascetic. In his wanderings, Confucius came across some of these who found shelter under the cloak of their self-isolation. They were scholars as was he, but they refused intercourse with him who went about from court to court endeavouring to find some influential centre from which he could apply his principles practically in the regulation of public affairs. They declared that no man desiring to live the life of a sage could remain in any court then existing.

He reasoned with his disciples on this matter. He could not convince himself that it was consistent with his duty to abandon all intercourse with his fellow-men and live for himself alone. The more widespread and violent were the evils of the time, the more clamant was the need for attempting their amendment. The sages and great men of old lived among the people to further their well-being, moral and physical. While he lived, he would endeavour to follow that example, and exert his utmost to reform and amend his generation. This he could do to a certain extent by ceaseless thought on the ethical principles which were the foundation of all good action, and by teaching these principles to the most talented young men who sought his instruction. But his hopes for a widespread reformation were centred on his becoming the " guide, philosopher, and friend " of the ruler of some State. Not for his own sake did he crave that position, but to obtain a coign of vantage wherefrom to exercise the greatest possible influence for the improvement of the condition of the people.

After the wide experience of a long life among all ranks
and conditions of men, he declared that he had ceased to
hope to see one worthy the name of sage. He would be
content if he met one who could be called " noble." The
way of the sage is so great as to be all but unattainable. The
sage does always the right thing intuitively and without
effort. Living a life in perfect accord with the " mean," he
is content to remain unacknowledged by, and unknown to,
the world. He is able to understand without difficulty, is
of clear discernment and extensive knowledge, fitted to be
the ruler of the nation. He is liberal, mild, gentle, tender,
able to exercise forbearance ; ready, energetic, firm, and
steadfast, able to hold his own ; orderly, grave, correct,
walking in the mean, able to command reverence ; cultured,
distinguished, particular in details, searching, able to exercise
judgment. Wide and extensive is he in his character like
Heaven, deep and vigorous like a fountain from the abyss.
All who see revere him ; all who hear believe him. His
actions give universal pleasure. His fame overspreads the
nation, and reaches to the barbarians beyond. Wherever ships
go and carriages run and man's strength can penetrate ;
where the heavens overshadow and the earth sustains ; where
the sun and moon shine, where frosts come and dews fall,
there all who have blood and breath honour and love him.
Therefore is he called the " Associate " of Heaven. The
Sage and the *Shen* can transform the world. A favourite
disciple asked whether the man should be called humane who
would confer benefits on every individual in the kingdom.
Confucius replied, " Why mention humaneness in a case like
that ? Such a man would be a sage. Even Yao and Shun
could only strive to do so much." This shows conclusively
the wholly practical character attributed to the sage by
Confucius.

Entertaining so high an ideal of the sage, it is not sur-
prising that he disclaimed the name for himself. He did not
hope ever to attain to it. All he could do was to learn without
weariness and to instruct without fatigue; and his life was
a ceaseless endeavour to attain to sagedom and humaneness.
The disciple responded that if he could learn without weariness
that showed his wisdom ; if he could teach without fatigue

that implied his humaneness. And the man who was both wise and humane possessed the character of the sage. In an apostrophe of admiration, Confucius exclaimed, " Great is the Way of the Sage! Like a flood it overflows and nourishes all things. In its height it reaches to heaven ; in extent it is complete, embracing all the three hundred rules of propriety and the three thousand of demeanour."

Exalted though the position be of the sage, Mencius declares that we are all of the same category. All men possess the natural endowments capable of leading them up to the lofty height, if they would but develop those endowments in regulating the thoughts of the heart and the deeds of their life. All men are of the same nature. The difference between the greatest sage and the ordinary man is that the sage is the first to see, to understand, and to practise in their completeness the principles inherent in every man. He is able to teach others to follow his example. Lack of will and effort are the sole obstacles to prevent any man from obtaining the position of the sage. The same was taught by a disciple of Confucius before Mencius was born. " Though the Tai mountain rises above the hills, it is still of the same nature as they. The Yellow River is greater than the stream in the valley, but it is of the same character. So the sage, though standing out conspicuous among men, is of the same nature as the common people. But from the beginning of mankind there never was so complete a man as Confucius." This disciple was probably the first who sounded so emphatically the note of the supereminence of his master.

In the definition of Mencius the sage transcends the noble man, and is but little inferior to the spirits of the sky, which affect us, though they are not understood by us.

CHAPTER VI.

THE NOBLE MAN.

The term *Chun* is commonly used throughout the classics to denote " Prince." But the term *Chuntsu* applies rather to character than to rank. It is variously translated, a common translation being " superior man." In its moral significance it stands contrasted with the " mean man." Hence the synonym adopted here is the " noble man." The ordinary use of this term is connected with birth rather than with merit. Happy the man to whom it can be applied in both senses. By Confucius the " mean man " is constantly brought forward antithetically with the apparent design of throwing the noble man into sharper relief, as a black ground increases the light of a bright picture.

Mencius gives an interesting list of ascending degrees of character. The man whose principles are self-educed and self-consistent is the Truthful man. He whose goodness is complete is Excellent. He whose goodness is illustrious is the Great or Noble man. He whose goodness is so great that it can influence and mould men is the Sage. He whose sagedom is beyond the understanding of man is *Shen*, or Spirit. The sage knows intuitively, his very presence moves kingdoms to goodness. He is rare in history as the phœnix. Next to him comes the noble man, who resembles the sage in wisdom and goodness, though to a lesser degree. His knowledge is acquired by assiduous study, and his goodness by incessant and earnest effort. His character is built up gradually, his reputation grows and spreads an increasing influence. He is a Great man who follows the great that is in him, and he is the mean man who pursues the mean. Some parts of man are noble ; others mean. He who nourishes the mean is a " small man." The senses do not think, and are easily misled by external things.

The mind thinks. Both mind and senses have been given by
Heaven. If man's nobler part be supreme, the inferior cannot
but follow. The man who is humane, loyal, and true, is the
noble of Heaven. The Duke, Marquis, and other ranks are
the nobles of earth. Such is the definition by Mencius of the
noble man.

Confucius usually defines the noble man by contrasting
to him the mean man. The noble man is affable but no
flatterer ; the mean man is a flatterer but not affable. He
is dignified without pride, the mean man proud without
dignity. He is easy to serve, but difficult to please, for what is
not right will not be pleasing to him. The mean man reverses
this character. He trusts in himself, the mean man in others.
He conceals his virtue though it becomes daily more brilliant,
the mean man seeks notoriety even when he is daily rushing
to ruin. He meditates on virtue, the mean man on land.
He thinks of law, the mean man on favours. He considers
integrity, the mean man profit. Continually he progresses
upward, the mean man downward. He is uniformly composed, the mean man is always in fear. He is liberal, but no
partisan, the mean man is a partisan but illiberal. He may
be distinguished in small affairs but may be trusted with
great, the mean man may not be entrusted with great affairs,
and he will be revealed in small. He sometimes fails in
humaneness, the mean man never has it. He may happen to
be in want, if the mean man is in want he resorts to lawlessness. The south is notable for teaching forbearance and
gentleness, and demands no revenge for unreasonable conduct. This is the way of the noble man who sets righteousness
above all. Valour in the noble man without righteousness
becomes mutinous, in the mean man it leads to robbery. In
his aims and desires he waits on the will of Heaven, the mean
man risks danger to hunt after luck. He stands in awe of
three things : (1) the Decree of Heaven, (2) the Great man,
(3) the Sayings of the Sage. The mean man does not know the
Decree of Heaven, therefore he cannot fear it, he is disrespect-
ful to great men and he ridicules the words of the sage.

He is anxious about truth, not about poverty. He is careful that the words he uses represent with the strictest accuracy
what he wishes to say, and that they correspond with his

deeds. Even in private he is solicitous about his conduct. He is cautious though he does not see, and earnest though he does not hear. He is therefore watchful of himself when no eye sees him. This self-cultivation of conduct is in reverence, hence he can give peace to the near and the far. His caution is not for a day, but for his entire life. Though but a country clown he thinks of the example of Shun, and desires always to rise to higher things. To him there is no such thing as calamity. What is calamity to ordinary men is no calamity to him, for his action is invariably in conformity with humaneness and propriety. It is indeed in this that he differs from other men. Humaneness and propriety rule his heart. The humane love men and the man of propriety respects men. He who loves men is beloved, and he is respected who respects others.

He knows neither grief nor fear. When self-examination discovers nothing wrong, why should he grieve or fear ? He does not murmur against Heaven, nor blame men. Though unacknowledged by men he is not annoyed. He is vexed because of his own lack of ability, not because men fail to recognise him. He is mild, but immovable in principle. He desires harmony, but is not facile. He is dignified, but will not wrangle ; sociable, but will be no partisan. He will study the fundamentals and apply them with all diligence to his conduct, so that his words are consistent with his deeds, and both in harmony with his position, whether it be low or high, rich or poor. He will not flatter those above nor despise those beneath him. While attending punctiliously to his public duties he will not forget those to his relatives. Pursuing human knowledge, he dare not neglect to learn to know Heaven.

He exerts his utmost to rectify defects which appear in his conduct, and to curtail excesses. He will not promote a man because of his words, nor neglect the words because of the man. He honours the worthy, is patient with all ; he praises the good and pities the incapable.

One put the question, " If the noble man possesses and practises the fundamentals, why should he trouble about culture and literature ? " He answered that both culture and literature were necessary and mutually helpful. The skin of a tiger or leopard without its hair was just like the skin of a sheep or a dog without its hair. He will use his culture to gain friends, and his friends to increase humaneness. It is by blending his culture and his principles into perfect harmony he becomes the noble man. He strives by intense study to gain the Way and make it his own that he may be kept from stumbling. Having made it completely his own, he makes it the dwelling-place of his mind where he has unbroken peace. He holds it with both hands, so that when others lose the little difference which distinguishes them from the birds and beasts he is able to stand. The greatness of his sphere of action will not increase his endowments, nor will poverty nor isolation diminish them. Even for the space of eating a meal he will not abandon virtue. When in haste he retains it, and in danger he will not forsake it. While government is properly conducted he will abide in office, but he will retire if it is bad. On account of his truthfulness the people will undertake labours which they would consider oppressive if ordered by one whom they did not trust ; and the sovereign will listen to advice which from another would be treated as libel. He will not support or oppose anything till he knows its rights. Even in face of death he will not change his principles.

He has his own special hates. He hates those who tattle about the evils of other people, who slander their superiors, and who display valour without propriety. If he is treated with perversity without apparent reason, he examines himself lest he may have given occasion for offence. He continues humane, and is persistently courteous. If the other is still obdurate he will conclude the case to be a hopeless one, that of a man without propriety, like the birds and the beasts. He will then decide to have no more to do with the fellow.

Though Confucius believed that all men possess the ability to act the noble man, he confessed that he himself came short of the ideal. The way of the noble man was easy to know, difficult to practise. It was far-reaching, yet secret. Common people knew it, but its fullness passes the understanding of the sage. Inferior people practise it, but its practice in perfection transcends the powers of the sage. As to its greatness, the whole world cannot contain it. It is so minute the whole world cannot subdivide it.

The noble man has three things against which to guard : when young and the passions not yet under control, he must guard against lust ; when in vigorous manhood, against pugnacity ; and when old and failing, against covetousness. Three things demand his particular attention : that his manner indicate no violence or heedlessness ; that the expression of his countenance be truthful ; and that no low or improper words escape his tongue. Nine things demand his constant care : that he see clearly when he looks ; hears accurately when listening ; shows a pleasant expression of face ; be respectful in manner; sincere in speech; devoted in business; that he inquire exhaustively when in doubt; realise the dangers connected with anger; and think of integrity in presence of gain.

CHAPTER VII.

ORIGIN OF THE SCRIPT OF CHINA.

The style of the literature of any country, and the character of it, provide a fair criterion of the civilisation of that country. Of the enormous dimensions of the literature of China it is not proposed here to treat. Nor is it possible to attempt to describe its character. But the script of China is so specially unique, its wonderful construction indicates so remarkable an inventiveness, and its combinations so much genius and logical arrangement, that a description of its origin is worthy of more attention than it has received in the west. Especially is this true when we reflect that it is involved in so much ignorance, and subject to so much misunderstanding, and even misrepresentation. Forty thousand different characters, representing as many words, all as distinctly different as the numerals of the west, claim examination as a mental marvel— or monstrosity if you will. But they enshroud the literature of the greatest number of readers of any one language. Its utility, as compared with the script of alphabetic letters used for the literatures of the rest of the world, is not now under consideration.

The principal authority on the forms and meanings of the early written characters of China is the dictionary called SHWO-WEN, or Treatise on Writing. It was compiled in the After-Han dynasty (25-250 A.D.). It was the work of a " forest " of learned men under the superintendence of one Hu. It is now published with an excellent commentary by the most eminent scholars of the ages following its production. It is a complete dictionary of all the ancient characters known. It is corroborated by the inscriptions on sacrificial and other vessels of bronze, specimens of which discovered in lakes, rivers, and upturned earth exist in large numbers. These shall be referred to later.

H

Chinese historians divide ancient times into three :—
(1) Early Ancient ; (2) Mid-Ancient ; (3) Late Ancient. Fuhi
is said to have ended the early and begun the mid-ancient
in B.C. 2950. Being endowed with keen powers of observation, he examined the figures of the heavens above, and
noted the forms of things on earth. From the outlines of
these he constructed the foundation for Chinese script. A
tortoise with marvellous markings on its back and a horse
with remarkable lines on its body came out of a river.
He copied them carefully, and from them made up the eight
diagrams which have played so great a part in Chinese life.
Shunnung (2737) is credited with devising a method for recording events by making knots of various sizes on cords.
Chinese critics agree that besides knotted cords there must
have been some other way of recording events before letters
were formed ; yet as letters were invented in the time of the
Five Emperors (2597-2205), how can Fuhi, they ask, be said
to have invented them ? Fuhi may be credited with the
formation of the eight diagrams by using long and
short lines, but, with the exception of such lines, he can
certainly not have discovered the method of writing the
Chinese characters.

After Fuhi, the name most prominently associated with
the invention of letters was Tsang Chie, secretary to Whang-ti
(2597). He is said to have studied the footprints made by
birds and beasts, the lines of feathers, of the human hand, etc.
By the combination of these he constructed the first characters. These were of simple construction, and of limited
extent. There were two varieties, both self-explanatory.
The first was made by the relative positions of lines, as —
one, and = two ; T below and ⊥ above. The second
class was pictorial, as ⊖ sun, ⟩ moon, 車 cart. The

first sort were called *Wen*, or tracings proper, the term still
used for literature. The second was called *Tsu*, or letters.
When they were once introduced, the characters spread
with great rapidity. But these two simple forms, though
adequate to explain the needs of a very primitive and limited
humanity, became quite inadequate to meet the demands of a
growing population and a rising civilisation. The demand was

met by combining the simple into compound forms, which provided for an indefinite supply. The characters thus supplied are divided into four classes. On Mount Taishan it was recorded that the complete evolution of the Chinese characters occupied the attention of the ablest minds for seventy-two generations, the last of whom was duke Chow.

These compound characters were of four classes. The first was called " substance-sound," an example of which is 江 the first part is " water," and the second *kung*, which merely lends its sound, the whole being *kiang*, " river." The second class is " combined-meaning." Here the two parts are necessary to indicate the new term, as 信. The first half is " man," the second is " word." A man standing beside his word is *sin*, truth or sincerity. The third class is called " comment-explanation." In this case the meaning of both parts is akin, the combination is intensive, as 狄 *li*, the first half is " dog," the second " fire." The combined word was the name of the ancestors of the ancient Huns, and was indicative of the fierceness of their disposition. Sun and moon placed side by side represented " brightness," physical and mental. The last class is termed " borrowing." When a character is required to express the name of a thing for which no written character exists, characters are borrowed having the same pronunciation, but with no reference to the meaning, as the city Lingchang, represented by the characters for *ling*. " command," and *chang*, " elder." The entire list of 40,000 characters is composed of the two simple and the four compound characters.

As the list of words was based on so arbitrary a foundation, confusion arose in course of time from variations in form or significance, which became so great that king Huen in B.C. 868 ordered his secretary to compile out of the chaotic mass a uniform system. It was known as Chwan characters, after the name of the secretary. Because it was largely used on seals, it came to be known as the " seal " character. Three centuries thereafter, Confucius used this form of character for his writings. The Chun chiw of Tso Chiwming was written in the same style. Not long after the time of Confucius, the first dictionary, called Urya, was issued to define the various characters. This was followed by many, of which the latest and best is the Shwo wen.

Towards the end of the Chow dynasty, China was divided into seventeen kingdoms, of which seven were of considerable extent. Though nominally subject to the suzerainty of Chow, these kingdoms were continually quarrelling. Each feudal prince adopted, discarded, modified the form, changed the pronunciation and meaning of old, and added new characters. This was done with the intention of creating confusion and independence. With the same design they changed the measures of length and capacity, the width of the cart axle so that the war chariots of one kingdom could not run in the ruts of another. Their hats and clothing were also made different, to distinguish the various kingdoms. When, after centuries of bloodshed among these Fighting Kingdoms, Chin shi whang displaced the Chow on the throne of China, welding the empire into a homogeneous whole, he introduced what was called a simpler mode of writing. This was called the "small seal," in contradistinction to the old, called the "large seal." The new system was the arrangement of his secretary, Li Szu. After the completion of this system, the Emperor ordered the exclusion of every character inconsistent with it. The use of the new system was made compulsory throughout the empire. He then ordered the disuse and destruction of all the old seal characters, and reduced to ashes all the ethical and political works of Confucius, which were the most formidable opponents of his methods of government. His Minister of Crime was a particularly busy man. Even the new seal character was to him a cumbersome method of writing out his numerous legal cases. He therefore invented another, which, from its form, was called the "square" form. With it he could write more rapidly. It came into general use, and is the character almost universally used to this day. A much abbreviated form was introduced in the Han dynasty, which succeeded the Chin. It is called the " grass " character, as it runs down cursively in a continuous line. It simplifies considerably the square form. Between the fullness of the square and the brevity of the grass writing stands the commercial hand. Except the last, these various characters are absolutely distinct, and require to be specially learned, as do our printed and written letters.

In the century preceding the Christian era, Kung, sovereign of the kingdom of Lu, now Shantung, desired to enlarge his palace. The house contiguous to the palace was that which had been the dwelling-place of Confucius. He purchased this house and pulled it down to extend the palace. In one of the partition walls were found copies of the following works, written in the large seal. The books were the Analects, Ritual, History, Chunchiw, Odes, and Filiality. By this discovery the lost large seal character was restored.

The number of characters in the first collection made in the ninth century before the Christian era was 3300. The compilation of Li Szu numbered 5340. In the sixth century A.D., under the Liang dynasty, the number had increased to 9353. Previous to that time, Examinations are supposed to have been inaugurated. The man who knew 9000 characters was appointed a Secretary of State, who had under him eighteen assistant secretaries. The number of characters continued to grow with the growth of the country, the increase of wealth, of possessions, and of knowledge. The great dictionary of Kanghi, called Tsuwhi, was published in 1699, and contained 33,179 words. And still the words went on increasing. In 1717 a completely new edition of that dictionary appeared. It was called Tsutien. This was followed by other editions. That in my possession has in round numbers 40,000 words.

The first books were made of bamboo slips six inches long strung together. Chin Shi whang introduced the use of silk as writing material. In his time books were divided into eight varieties : (1) the ancient seal ; (2) the small seal ; (3) bamboo slips ; (4) insect forms for flags and banners ; (5) seals for stamping ; (6) office books and libraries ; (7) writings

on war ; (8) writings on crime.   Several centuries afterwards, when the language was fairly well established, books
were divided into six classes : (1) the ancient seal, discovered
in the house of Confucius ; (2) ancient seal different from
the first, discovered in times more recent ; (3) small seal ; (4)
square character ; (5) seal for stamping ; (6) representations
of birds and insects for banners.

When the short-lived dynasty of Chin had passed away, a
strong re-action set in favouring the restoration of Confucianism. This feeling was kindled to enthusiasm by the discovery
of his books in the demolished wall of his house.   These
were deciphered within the century preceding the Christian
era by Kung Ankwo, a descendant of Confucius.   The general
interest set men a-thinking, and some a-plotting.   After the
destruction of those books, scholarly men who had committed
them to memory recited them, or portions of them, to their
descendants.   Many characters differing in form were pronounced the same.   Others similar in form differed in pronunciation.   From both of these differences, errors arose in transmission from father to son.   These errors were unintentional,
and were not difficult to trace.   Considerable confusion in
the writing of the classics resulted, which has provided abundant
occupation for able editors from that day to this.   Many of
the errors were corrected by the discovery of the books in the
wall.   In the fashionable craze after that discovery, clever
and unscrupulous men, who have existed in China as in other
lands, found their opportunity.   And as handsome rewards
were offered to all who discovered new characters, not a few
books were discovered which had never existed, but were the
product of forgery.

In a rainless climate like that of Egypt, books of many
centuries old may be conserved, but in a rainy climate like
that of China this could not be rationally expected.   The
Han dynasty made paper of grass, and subsequently paper
was made of the inner skin of the poplar tree.   But it is in-
conceivable that books, either of bamboo, of silk, of grass, or
the poplar tree, if exposed to the weather or under the earth,

could have survived to the present day. Books nine centuries
old I have seen, but these were carefully preserved in human
habitations. In any book now existing we have therefore
only problematical evidence of the primitive forms of Chinese
writing.

But if we have not in books absolute proof, we have in
bronzes evidence galore. The only temples existing in early
days were those devoted to the worship of ancestors. The
reigning ruler, whether of the empire or of a state, was obliged
to possess such a temple. In these temples offerings were
presented at stated times to ancestral spirits of meat, fish,
fruit, grain, and libations of spirits. Each variety of offering
required a distinctive sort of vessel. This involved vessels
many in number and of great variety. At these offerings
feasts for the relatives of the dead, to whom the offerings were
presented, had to be provided and other sets of vessels, both
for eating and drinking, were required. It is recorded that
the earliest vessels were made of earthenware. These were
pricked all over with figures, each with special significance in
honour of the person to whom the offering was presented.
The next step was their manufacture in wood. Gold and
jade were also used. In the Shang dynasty (B.Ç. 1766-1123),
metal began to be used for these sacrificial vessels. The
offerings were presented to ancestors of the five preceding
generations. For a newly-deceased ancestor new vessels
were prepared. The first of the five ancestors was always the
founder of the family. The next was invariably changed
with every new addition, so that there were always five. The
sovereign used nine vessels of each kind, the feudal princes
seven, the high officials five, and other officials three. All
this makes it abundantly clear that after the introduction of
metal vessels the number in existence became very great. The
vessels of the sovereign were of gold, those of princes of silver,
those of high officials of copper, and those of other officials and
literary men of iron. In the palace of Mukden are specimens
of the Shang dynasty, but many more of the Chow. There
are also beautiful specimens made in the beginning of the

Manchu dynasty of cloisonné after the pattern of the ancient
vessels.

With every change of dynasty, there was a complete change
of the sacrificial vessels. It is thus readily understood how
in dynasties subsequent to those who had made the earliest
vessels, there were discovered in lakes, in rivers, in up-turned
earth, and on mountain sides large numbers of old, effete,
and discarded sacrificial vessels. The graceful lines and beautiful workmanship of those vessels are remarkable and worthy
of notice. But for us the fact of greatest importance connected with the vessels is that inscriptions in the contemporary script were engraved on great numbers of even the
oldest.

Of those ancient bronzes thousands of specimens remain.
Their inscriptions have been deciphered as far as the characters were recognisable. Here we have the unquestioned
evidence of the ancient forms of Chinese characters, not from
books, which, because of frequent transmission, were liable
to change, but from the actual engraved words of thirty-six
centuries ago. For knowledge of the earliest forms of script,
we are indebted to the learned men of the Sung dynasty, many
of whom made these inscriptions the study of their life. With
singular ability and devotion, they deciphered and carefully
delineated the curious inscriptions. The results of their
learned labour were published in A.D. 1119. The noble work,
beautifully done, was in thirty volumes, and entitled " Po-
ku-tu," or " Investigation of Ancient Drawings." A copy of
the work was in my possession issued in 1529. With many
another old book, this was burnt by the Boxers. I was,
fortunately, able to replace it by another copy issued in 1603,
at which date the last edition of that particular work was
issued. In these volumes the vessels are represented in careful outline. The inscriptions are in exact facsimile, with the
corresponding modern characters underneath. The date, dimensions, weight, and uses of the vessels are clearly detailed.
In this reproduction of the ancient script, we see the exact form
of writing in use centuries before Confucius. An important

work supplementing the Po-ku-tu, and going over the same period, is the " Si-ching-ku-chien," or " West Clear Mirror of Antiquity." It is an imperial folio edition prepared and printed for the emperor Kienlung. It too is a beautiful work, done in the best style of Chinese art. It is of forty large volumes, with two additional devoted to coins. As in Po-ku-tu, the date, weight, and dimensions of the outlined vessels are noted, but for their uses reference is made to Po-ku-tu. This great work was gifted by the Emperor and his successors to friends, or to men who were specially distinguished for important services to their country. A third work, " Kin-shi-so," or " Records from Metal and Stone," was issued in 1822. It supplies specimens of the very ancient vessels with their inscriptions. But its chief value consists in the reproduction of scenes and writings on metal, and especially on stone, the production of artists of the Han period, about the beginning of the Christian era. The scenes depicted are of peace and war, of fishing and cooking, of driving and dressing, with numerous illustrations of prominent historical figures. A laughing imagination guided the pencil which originated, and artistic gifts the chisel which sculptured, the figures. In these three works there are specimens of the script of the Shang dynasty, in not a few of which can be traced the original, out of which were evolved the more elaborate characters of the seal of Chow.

The characters on the vessels of Shang were frequently but one, and always very few. They were largely composed of a few strokes outlining an animal, or other object, emblematic of the person in whose honour the vessel was made. The number of characters was limited, and from their nature few presented any difficulty to the deciphering skill of the Sung scholars. But pictorial representation of words could not fail to prove inadequate for the purpose of writing.

With the Chow dynasty a great change was introduced. At first the Shang character continued naturally to assert its influence. But in course of time the more elaborate seal character took entire possession of the domain of the pen. It was both a complicated and an arbitrary system. But the words were greatly multiplied. The inscriptions on the vessels became enlarged, and sometimes gave historical incidents. The Sung scholars found greater difficulty in deciphering the seal of the Chow than the pictorial words of Shang. In the longer inscriptions of Chow, many characters were beyond the learned skill of Sung. The inscriptions are fully and carefully copied, but in not a few instances a cipher represents a character which baffled the scholars. Specimens will illustrate this testimony to their honesty.

Two conclusions follow from the careful study of the inscriptions on those bronzes. The first is that whether a man called Fuhi did or did not exist, whether he did or did not take the first steps in raising the Chinese out of barbarism, he certainly did not originate the Chinese written characters. By the use of long and short lines he may have formed the eight diagrams, but whatever the utility might have been of these, they have no affinity with Chinese ancient characters. They are absolutely straight lines. Examination of the specimens of Chinese characters of the oldest times will show them to be essentially of curved lines. Between the time ascribed to Fuhi and the Shang dynasty there were, as Chinese writers think, probably other modes of recording events than knotted cords. There may have been the crude beginnings of writing by pictorial representation such as is characteristic of Shang. In the middle of the Chow dynasty a collection was formed of Chinese characters, and the number then in use was 3300. We may rest assured that even of that limited number, not one was known to Fuhi two thousand years before.

The other conclusion is that the rise of the Chinese language is, like that of the people, indigenous. The beginnings of Chinese script were of the simplest and rudest, and they were very few. From the few lines scratching a rude representation of a tiger, of a tree, or of growing grain to the evolution of a universally recognised seal character in the middle of the Chow dynasty there elapsed the period of a thousand years. The original word pictorially indicating some object became modified, sometimes beyond recognition, but its pronunciation and significance remained practically the same as they do to this day.   It has to be noted, however, that no book was written on pronunciation till a few centuries after the Chow dynasty. But, as the formation of words and the grammatical construction of the sentence was the same in the Chow and in subsequent dynasties, it is legitimate to infer that both pronunciation and meaning were practically the same in both instances.

One peculiarity of the Chinese language is the manner in which compound words are formed from simple, the various compounds having a pronunciation and meaning different from any of the simple factors, yet retaining some allusion to them.   Take as illustrations a few examples from the three simple words " water," " wood," " fire " :—

Water, 水 *shui.*   Another form,

Wood, 木 *mu.*

Fire, 火 *huo.*   Another form, **''''**

Water duplicated, 沝 *chui*, water.

Water tripled, 淼 *miao*, vastness of the sea.

Water with wood, 沐 *mu,* to bathe.

Water with wood duplicated, 淋 *lin,* dropping as water from roof.

Wood duplicated, 林 *lin,* a forest.

Wood trebled, 森 *shen,* overgrown with wood.

Wood with fire underneath, 杰 *chie,* a hero.

Wood duplicated with fire, 焚 *fen,* set on fire.

Fire duplicated, 炎 *yen,* flame, glorious,

Fire trebled, 焱 *yen,* brilliant.

Fire duplicated with water, 淡 *tan,* watery, insipid.

For other examples of the manipulation of one character in order to produce an indefinite number of new words and meanings, see in Section III. the character for " man." Thus it is manifest that there is practically no end to the possible combinations of Chinese words.

Except by two ancient kingdoms in Manchuria, and by the Japanese, Chinese words have not, like Babylonian and Egyptian, been used as letters or syllables. In Kanghi's dictionary two words are used as phonetics, one to give the beginning of the pronunciation of a new word, and the second to give its termination. These two words have nothing to do with the meaning of the new word.

Even among well-informed men, there exists a suspicion, sometimes a belief, that between Sumerian and the Chinese languages there is so close a resemblance that the former is likely to have been the model on which the latter was based. For the sake of my reading of Chinese literature it is, therefore, necessary to examine that suspicion more minutely.

The oldest known script of Babylonia was in straight lines representing parts of the human body, of animals, of plants, natural and manufactured articles. These lines are traceable to an age supposed to have been about B.C. 6000. They represent a language which is Turanian like Turkish or Mongol. It was the language of the oldest known residents of Babylonia. It did not possess words for " horse," " lion," " vine," " fig," which are objects well known in Babylonia ; the inference is that their forefathers went from some other land into Babylon. This land was supposed to be Elam, for their word for country is the same as for " east " and " mountain."

One section called Sumer occupied the marshy lands at the head of the Persian Gulf. Those on the extreme north of the plain were known as Akkads, from the name of their capital, Agade. Though one people, they were usually two Powers. Even at that early date, they possessed a highly developed civilisation, which could have been attained only as the result of a prolonged experience. Had they been nomads in their original home, like the Chow and the Chin, they might have wandered westwards into the rich plain of Babylonia, and there have begun a life of agriculture, necessitating, as in the case of China, a system of writing of some kind.

In that rainless country they instituted irrigation by the regulation of rivers, the cutting of canals, and the use of pumping machines. By a marvellous system of canalisation they, in the sixtieth century B.C., drained the pestiferous marshes, and converted them into fertile lands. They built fortresses, cities of brick, temples which were the centres of population, made vases of clay, and invented a system of writing on wood by pictorial outlines of the objects represented. When these words were written on clay, and subsequently baked, the lines became slightly changed, whence arose the cuneiform or wedge-shaped lines. The change simplified the manner and extended the use of the writing. The pictorial words fell into desuetude except for theological and legal writings. By the year B.C. 3800, when Sargon established the first great Semitic kingdom, he adopted the cuneiform writing, which had been perfected centuries before his time, and the pictorial form was discarded.

For centuries before Sargon the Semites had made incursions against Akkad. They were rude barbarians compared to the Akkadians, whose civilisation they borrowed. Akkad ultimately fell before these repeated attacks. Sargon subdued them completely, annexing them to his own Semitic people. He adopted to its full extent the civilisation of the Sumerians, and extended it. Under him artistic talent produced articles of such beauty as has not been excelled. He extended the bounds of his kingdom to the coast of the Mediterranean, and over the whole introduced the use of the cuneiform letters. This form of writing was known even in Egypt. He raised the Semitic kingdom to a high state of civilisation and organisation. He set up judges and made good roads. The people of Akkad were absorbed, and their language became lost in the Semitic. In 2850 the last Akkadian had disappeared.

The name of Babylon had not then emerged. Its first king set up his throne in 2450. The great Khamurabbi dates from 2342. Thirty years thereafter, Sumeria on the south was absorbed, and Babylon became one united kingdom. The union was followed by a high state of civilisation, accompanied by great prosperity.

Contemporary with the Shang dynasty in China, the Kassites, a rude people from Elam, with an agglutinative language, became the rulers of Babylon. They adopted the civilisation of the conquered. Thereafter the Sumerians were completely amalgamated. Their language and nationality were submerged, and the various races were welded into one Babylonian people. As appears above, the Chinese people and empire passed through a similar experience.

Sculptures subsequent to 4000 B.C. indicate two distinct races in the land of Babylon. One was a long-headed, long-bearded race, unmistakably Semitic. The other was a round-headed, beardless race, with prominent cheek bones and shaven crowns, represented as the conquered race. These latter were the early inhabitants who had developed so remarkable a civilisation. In Elam was another such race found, round-headed and beardless, but destitute of civilisation till they had borrowed from the Sumerians. The Finnish tribes, from Finland, in north-eastern Europe, along the north of Asia to the Samoyedes in the north-east, were of a similar race, and spoke the same kind of language. The language of eastern Turanians bore no trace of any other language than their own. Not a particle of evidence exists to show any connection between the Turanians, who occupied from the earliest the lands of Shensi, and those in western Asia. That there may have been some communication between the inhabitants east and west of the Tienshan is probable, though there is no sort of evidence. Eastern Thibet and Szuchen were in the most ancient times known to the Chinese. They were then also of the same race and language as the other Turanians.

The entire country from the Tienshan to the Yellow River was inhabited by the nomadic barbarians. They were

divided into numerous kingdoms or tribes, all warlike, all
jealous of encroachment by neighbouring kingdoms or tribes,
all tending their own sheep, oxen, horses, and dogs, all within
their strictly-defined limits, on to which no other was permitted to trespass. To the east of these were the Chinese
agriculturists, with physical characteristics similar to their
western neighbours, but with manners and modes of life of
quite another order. We may therefore infer that though
the Chinese differed socially they were of the same race as
the nomads. Therefore the whole population of northern Asia
were racially and linguistically probably of the same race as
the early inhabitants of Babylon. The only exception of which
we know anything were the hairy Oinos in the north-east of
Manchuria.

Thus we perceive that from the Yellow River at Shansi
westward into central Asia, numerous nomadic kingdoms and
fierce tribes presented a dead and impassable wall to the Chinese
if they should entertain any notion of going westwards. But
they were then a small nation, a poor people, occupied with
the incessant demands of their fields, and lacking opportunity
or desire to travel beyond their own cultivated property, and
glad if they could only have peace within their own borders.
They knew of no inducement, social, intellectual, or religious, to
leave their own land. There was nothing in the west to attract
them. It was after the absorption of the whole of nomadic
Shensi into the kingdom of Chin that westward movements
became possible to the rapidly growing people of China. It was
the Han dynasty, after many years of fierce fighting, which first
found its way through eastern Thibet into central Asia. The
Kitan nomads were driven by their kindred Huns from the
west of the Yellow River to south-west Manchuria, where, after
the lapse of centuries, they founded the kingdom of Liao.
This dynasty extended its sway over north China, embracing
all north of the Yellow River. They too penetrated by war
into central Asia, whither they themselves were finally driven
by the Kin dynasty, which took its rise in north-eastern
Manchuria. Even at so late a date, when knowledge had

increased, communication between China and the west was of the most meagre and unfriendly description. Previous to the full development of Chinese language, literature, and civilisation, it was physically impossible for the Chinese even to know of the existence of Babylon, far less possible was it to have any sort of intercourse with it. And it must on the other hand be remembered that Babylon had no concern with anything east of Elam. The politically gravitating influence on Babylon was not from the far east, but was in and from the west, and centred in Egypt.

When the Sumerians were at the height of their civilisation, after they had discarded the pictorial for the cuneiform writing, the ancestors of the Chinese were savages, living on or under trees in summer, and in pits in winter to escape the cold. Their food was uncooked. They were ignorant of the use of fire and of clothing. Needless to say, they were not in a position to think of letters, whether pictorial or other. These savages were not one whit superior when Sargon in 3800 was establishing his kingdom from the Tigris to the Mediterranean. Long after the pictorial writing of the Sumerians had become a thing of the past, the Chinese are said to have been recording events by the use of knotted cords. And centuries after the cuneiform had completely supplanted the pictorial in Babylon, Fuhi was taking the first elementary steps in the elevation from barbarism of the Chinese, and framing his long and short lines into the eight diagrams. The first attempt at the formation of Chinese characters is ascribed to Whang-ti, if ever there was such a man. His date is given as the twenty-sixth century B.C., thirteen centuries after Sargon, in whose time the cuneiform alphabetic form had been the long-established form of writing. If the Chinese writing began then, it certainly did not begin any sooner. From the paucity and rudeness of the characters in the early Shang dynasty in the eighteenth century, it appears to me that the very earliest attempts at writing intelligible words cannot have preceded the Hia dynasty, or about the twentieth century B.C. Even in the ninth century, when the first collection was made of

Chinese written words, there were only 3300 words constructed. At least thirty centuries before that time the cuneiform was a perfected system universally used from the Tigris to Egypt, and the pictorial had been discarded. Had the Chinese been in a position to borrow a system of writing in the twentieth century, why should they adopt a few strokes or signs from the pictorial system discarded twenty centuries before, and refuse to adopt the perfected, alphabetic system then in universal use in the west ? It should not be forgotten that the Sumerian characters were written in straight lines, and those of China in curves. Straight lines, or the square character, came into existence in China under Chin Shi Whang, and any document, book, or bone with square characters is of necessity subsequent to that date. At the time when pictorial writing was used in Sumeria, China could not go to the west and Babylonia did not desire to come east. From the impracticability of intercourse arising from the physical difficulties interposed by space, and the still greater difficulties interposed by time, the theory of the Babylonian source of the Chinese language is absurdly impossible, nor is it necessary to discuss it further.

But the impossibility of that theory does not preclude the possibility of some resemblance between the pictorial writing of the Sumerians and that of China. The two peoples, though separated by an interval of four thousand years, were alike industrious agriculturists working in rich soil. Both grew grain of various sorts, were surrounded by water, by trees, and by flora. They were acquainted with animals, domestic and wild. They passed their life in practically the same circumstances. We should be surprised, therefore, not that there should happen to be a few instances of similarity in their pictorial languages, but that there should have been none. In the preceding pages two principles are specified on which the first characters were formed, one being the relative position of strokes, the other a rude outline of the object signified. The number of characters possible by this method is limited,

I

and indicates the poverty of the people and the narrowness of their possessions.

In Stein's "Kotan" are found numerous illustrations of wreckage discovered in the ruins of the sand-covered cities of central Asia. On both wood and paper are many examples of Chinese writing, all of which are in the modern square and cursive hands. There is no example of the old seal character, nor of the older pictorial. There are illustrations of cash discovered in the ruins. They are of the Tang and Sung dynasties, without any specimen of the Han dynasty. One coin had the legend *wuchu* in seal characters. The legend refers to the weight of the coin. The first coin of this description was minted in B.C. 118, the last in A.D. 713-741. During all that period coins were issued with those two characters, many of them showing variations, not one of which is represented in the list from "Khotan." The date of that particular coin cannot, therefore, be decided. But the fact that it was found along with numerous Tang and Sung cash proves that its presence there is no evidence of an age anterior to Tang. Great quantities of Tang cash have been found in Manchuria, left there subsequent to the expulsion by Tang of the Koreans. The interesting discoveries in "Khotan" have but a negative bearing on the relation between China and Babylon ; but the inference derived is the negation of any intercourse with central Asia before the Han period. In "Khotan," accurate references are made to the statements in Chinese history on the connection with the west. That connection began with the Han dynasty.

SECTION III.—REPRODUCTION OF SCRIPT.

CHAPTER I.

INSCRIPTIONS ON VESSELS.

In times antecedent to their written history, the Chinese believed in, and evidenced great reverence for One Supreme Being, whom they worshipped as Creator and Preserver of men. But, strange to say, they have never had a temple dedicated to His service. Even now the so-called temple in Peking is an altar, not a temple. Beside this altar, and in connection with it, is a magnificent platform open to the heavens on which worship is performed. Being everywhere present, He could be worshipped anywhere. As Abraham erected an altar wherever he happened to sojourn, so the Chinese rulers in remote history erected an altar to the Supreme Ruler whereever they happened to set up a camp. But nowhere throughout the ages has there been a covered-in temple for the Supreme (" Original Religion of China ").

The Chinese have always displayed a particular reverence for parents, especially after their decease. The first duty of the founder of a new dynasty was to erect a temple in his capital to the memory of his parents and their preceding ancestors to the fifth generation. This temple was more or less ornate, and was always roofed to protect it from wind and rain. In this, as at the altar, there was no image. In commemoration and honour of the ancestors there were fixed services at the beginning of each of the four seasons, besides occasional services for all great public events, either already consummated or proposed.

For these services special vessels, of which there was great variety and large numbers, were prepared. The offerings consisted of all sorts of meat, of fish, of grain, of vegetables, of fruit, and of liquor. For each kind there was a separate vessel, distinctive in shape, size, and number. The first vessels were said to have been of clay. The Hia dynasty introduced the use of wood. These vessels, cut to pattern, were pricked all over with figures which indicated the person in whose honour the service was held. The figures were partly arbitrary, but mostly of pictorial outlines, roughly drawn to represent some quality of the deceased. A spear, a sword, a bow and arrow indicated one famed in war. The four-and-half centuries during which the Hia ruled were adequate to stereotype the fashion of such outlines and to attach a particular meaning to each. Improvements were effected in the shape of the vessel and the contour of the emblem. Their limited sphere in temple use made the emblems familiar, and, whether they were merely suggestive or pictorial, they were soon practically converted into words. The plurality of persons honoured in worship necessitated differentiating emblems, which were also in the course of generations used as words with definite meanings. Those best known and always used became less formal and intricate, and gradually forsook the pictorial outlines. I have searched in vain for authentic specimens of Hia inscriptions. But we are justified in supposing that they are found in the earliest inscriptions of the Shang. Among the pictorial words in Shang are not a few which either never were pictorial, or had become so simplified as to suggest no picture.

The decadent dynasty of Hia passed away, and with it the vessels of wood. The Shang dynasty replaced these by vessels of metal. But though the material was changed, we are distinctly told that in the vessels of Shang and of Chow we behold the most ancient forms. As some of the earliest inscriptions of Shang present elaborate words which are decidedly not pictorial, we are justified in believing that the process of developing pictorial into more formal words had at least begun in the preceding reign. Whether it was in this fashion or from the uncommon ability of Tang, it so happened, that in the early Shang dynasty, there were not a few words which bore no trace of the pictorial. Preceding generations of reverential worshippers would have popularised many emblems of royalty which the newly established dynasty would adopt. During the long period of six-and-a-half centuries over which Shang reigned, there was ample opportunity and many occasions for further development from the pictorial. Of this development there is abundant evidence in the greatly extended and more elaborate script of the early Chow as compared with that of the early Shang.

One distinctive feature of the Shang is that the inscriptions are particularly brief, frequently of only two characters, and not seldom of but one. This feature is manifest in the long list of Shang inscriptions reproduced below. The same is said to have been true of the Hia. In the Chow dynasty there is no instance of one or of two words, while there are many instances of hundreds. Specimens are given below.

The later Chow script was as different from the early as the early was from that of the Shang. The inscription on the *ting* dedicated to king Wen by duke Chow is exactly like the script of Shang. The modification, if any, is so slight as to be inappreciable. There is, however, a rapidly increasing difference in style in the second century after the Chow had settled down and devoted their attention to literature. Four centuries after the enthronement of Chow, the method of writing became more free, the use of pictorial emblems became more and more limited, till they gradually disappeared. The number of characters rapidly increased, and a great impetus was given to writing. The bronze inscriptions became at once more literary, more varied, and more full. Then began the real creation of literature in China.

The sacrificial offerings were invariably accompanied by a feast for all the members of the family then gathered together. The close association of sacrifice and feast was perhaps the reason why, in the Shang period, the same vessels were usable for both. The Chow made a sharp distinction between the two, those for use at the sacrifices being regarded as more sacred. Hence the same sort of vessel was sometimes known by different names according to the purpose for which it was used.

When a novel and startling theory is announced which appears to be antagonistic to theories previously in vogue, incontrovertible proofs are demanded in its support. The facts and reasons already adduced may be proof adequate to most readers that the theory of this book has been fully established; but destructive criticism may not be satisfied with reproductions of supposed inscriptions on vessels purporting to be of the Shang dynasty. To meet their claim, another line of proof may be enunciated bearing on the authenticity of the Shang inscriptions. The most conclusive evidence of age would be dates recorded in the body of the inscription on the vessel. These are common in the oldest inscriptions of the Chow dynasty. On the Shang vessels I have been able to discover only one date. The vessel is dedicated to the memory of an elder brother, and is the only one of the kind. It is peculiar also in the two final words. It is solitary in giving an unknown historical allusion. In it occurs the phrase " ninth year of the king." Now, the term for " year " was different in different epochs. King Yao called it " Tsai," Hia dynasty called it " Swi," Shang called it " Szu," and Chow called it " Nien." The term used in the above phrase is " szu," proving it to have been engraved in the Shang dynasty. Kwei was the term always applied to the father of Tang, who was the founder of the dynasty. It appears alone on one vessel, and in combination with other words on others. In one instance a grandson of Fu Kwei holds a spear. Kwei is several times represented as holding a spear. Such a vessel was made by a grandson, or other descendant, while the first was made by Tang himself, as was his duty on his attaining the throne.

The title Fu Ren provides a near approximation to a date. Among the rulers was a Chung Ren whose son was Tai Kia, and a Wai Ren whose son was Tsu Yi.

The vessel on which father Ren is engraved must have been made either by Tai Kia or Tsu Yi. Tsu Sin, called the fourteenth ruler of Shang, was son of this Tsu Yi, older brother of Wu Kia, and father of Tsu Ting. He is represented as a man holding wood or a spear, both of which were used in the dances which accompanied the great sacrifices in the time of Shang and the beginning of Chow. All these names are represented on the vessels. They are all names of Shang rulers, and of them only, and stand for a certain definite period in the dynasty.

The Shu, or Book of History, had obtained its final form centuries before the recovered bronzes had attracted the attention of scholars to their remarkable inscriptions. It has been mentioned that even after many years of study by the keen minds of the learned men of Sung, there remained not a few emblems untranslatable. Thus was manifested their great age and also their desuetude. All this was equally true of the Chow characters as of the pictorial words of Shang. But the person to whom the vessel was dedicated was indicated on every Shang vessel, even when the inscription consisted only of one character.

Now, the Shu was chiefly if not entirely compiled by Confucius, and contains a complete list of the twenty-eight rulers of the Shang dynasty. It is worth while to give this list in its chronological order :—The first is Tang, the Complete, who founded the dynasty. He is known as Tien Yi. The second is Tai Kia ; the third, Wu Ting ; the fourth, Tai Keng ; the fifth, Siao Kia ; the sixth, Yung Ki ; the seventh, Tai Mao ; the eighth, Chung Ting ; the ninth, Wai Ren ; the tenth, Ho Tan Kia ; the eleventh, Tsu Yi ; the twelfth, Tsu Sin ; the thirteenth, Wu Kia ; the fourteenth, Tsu Ting ; the fifteenth, Nan Keng ; the sixteenth, Yang Kia ; the seventeenth, Pan Keng ; the eighteenth, Siao Sin ; the nineteenth, Siao Yi ; the twentieth, Wu Ting ; the twenty-first, Tsu Keng ; the twenty-second, Tsu Kia ; the twenty-third, Ling Sin ; the twenty-fourth, Keng Ting ; the twenty-fifth, Wu Yi ; the twenty-sixth, Tai Ting ; the twenty-seventh, Ti Yi ; the twenty-eighth, Chow Sin.

Among the selections given below by reproduction of the Shang inscriptions it will be noted that there is no instance

of the first word in any of the above pairs, except the word
Tsu, which was at once a personal name and the Chinese for
" ancestor," in which sense it is used throughout the inscriptions. But there are numerous instances of the second word
of the pair. The reason is that the first is the personal de-
signation and the second the title. The first is replaced by
the word " father," " mother," grandfather," or some other
personal relation. No name appears on the bronzes. The
person to whom the vessel is dedicated is indicated by the title
and the donor by his blood relationship. When the word
" father " is engraved on the vessel it is evident that it was
made by the son ; the name of the father does not occur.
When we have the title " father Yi " on the vessel, we know
that the title of the father was *yi*. But there are half-a-dozen
of this title. The affix *yi* was attached to six persons. The
first was Pao Yi, who was the fourth generation of the ancestors of Tang. The second was Tang himself, known as
Tien Yi. The third was Tsu Yi, the fourteenth generation
from Tang. Then came Siao Yi, Wu Yi, and Ti Yi. On
each of the vessels dedicated to all these the inscription would
be " Fu Yi " or " father " *yi*, without any distinguishable
difference to indicate the particular " father " referred to.
The various vessels were, however, different in their ornamentation. This was sometimes of clouds, sometimes of
thunder, sometimes of dragons, and sometimes of gluttony.
Probably the vessels could be distinguished at the time of using
them by their particular ornamentation. The inscriptions
Fu Kia and Fu Ting were equally numerous, and might represent any one of various individuals.

In the Shu there is the full name and title of all the Shang
rulers. On the vessel the name does not occur, but the final
word of the title is engraved. These final words are borrowed
from what are called the Ten Stems, and this borrowing is
characteristic of Shang and of no other dynasty. Each of
the rulers assumed one of the ten stems as his title.

The reproductions which follow are merely specimens ;
there are many more inscriptions of the Shang dynasty of a

similar type. The selection given should afford proof adequate
of the authenticity of both the Shu, which records the public
history of Shang, giving the names, and of the unearthed
vessels which supply the titles of the rulers for a totally
different purpose and in an entirely independent form. The
two sources of information provide mutual corroboration
which is remarkable, and in which there is no possibility of
collusion. In these facts, from the combined evidence of
Book and Bronze, we have undoubted proof of authenticity.

The Ten Stems which had been adopted as part of their
title by the Shang rulers were used, from some period of the
unknown past, combined in pairs to indicate the five elements.
With the twelve Branches they formed pairs which numbered
successive days, and at the time of Han began to mark the
cycle of sixty years, making an accurate method of chronology.
The Ten Stems are :—First, *Kia*, a bud, the first ; second,
yi, a final particle, completion ; third, *ping*, bright ; fourth,
ting, adult, a person ; fifth, *wu*, luxuriant ; sixth, *ki*, self,
central ; seventh, *keng*, metal ; eighth, *sin*, acrid, pungent ;
ninth, *ren*, great ; tenth, *kwei*, consider. The odd numbers
are all *yang* and the even all *yin*. The first pair denotes
wood and the east, the second pair fire and the south, the
third pair earth, the fourth pair metal, the north-east, and
the west ; the fifth water and the north.

The twelve branches are :—First, *tsu ;* second, *chou ;*
third, *yin ;* fourth, *mao ;* fifth, *chen ;* sixth, *szu ;* seventh,
wu ; eighth, *wei ;* ninth, *shen ;* tenth, *yu ;* eleventh, *su ;*
twelfth, *hai*. These divide the twenty-four hours thus : the
first, 12–1 a.m. ; second, 1–3 a.m. ; third, 3–5 a.m. ; fourth,
5–7 a.m. ; fifth, 7–9 a.m. ; sixth, 9–11 a.m. ; seventh, 11–1
p.m. ; eighth, 1–3 p.m. ; ninth, 3–5 p.m. ; tenth, 5–7 p.m. ;
eleventh, 7–9 p.m. ; twelfth, 9–11 p.m.

To produce the cycle of sixty years each of the ten stems
is paired with each of the branches, both in regular succession,
as *tsukia, chou yi*, etc., six successions of the stems and five
of the branches complete the cycle of sixty years and admit
of no confusion.

The subjects covered by the numerous bronze vessels of Shang are limited to sacrifice and feasting. Hence the inscriptions are also limited. They are dedicated to family relatives and some prominent officials. The terms " son," " grandson," "ancestor," "father" occur continually. Those showing variations of form are given. While much material is omitted, everything is presented which had any bearing on the construction or development of the script. An explanation of the inscriptions or of the shapes and uses of the vessels is impossible in a work like this, which is devoted to the history of the construction at its earliest known period of the Chinese script.

The first duty of the founder of a dynasty having been to erect in honour of his ancestors a temple with appropriate sacrificial vessels, we are justified in believing that some of the inscriptions date from the very beginning of the Shang dynasty. The names of some of the kings associated with the ten stems represent its concluding years. The lapse of six centuries indicates little change in the outlines of the characters. Almost all the characters of the Shang inscriptions, except the pictorial, are frequently repeated in long and numerous inscriptions of the first century and half of the Chow dynasty.

CHAPTER II.

FUHI.

Fuhi is the most ancient name mentioned by Confucius, and is the reputed originator of the first steps from barbarism to Chinese civilisation. Chinese historians give him the credit of laying the foundation of Chinese script. We may ascribe to him the honour of instituting marriage and the rudiments of social life. But from what appears above, in the examination of the origin of Chinese script, it is impossible to credit him with the construction of even the beginnings of the written characters of China. The eight diagrams in long and short lines are ascribed to him. From two bronze vessels of the Shang dynasty represented below, examples of the eight diagrams are proved to have existed before the Chow dynasty. These differ from the set of diagrams usually represented, but the difference is not radical. He may have used long and short scratches to denote some sort of meaning. But the significance attached to these in modern times never entered the imagination of Fuhi or other leader of the people for a thousand years after him. The *yang* and *yin* theory was introduced into the philosophy of China at the end of the twelfth century B.C. Though the straight line is an absolute stranger to the earliest characters in the oldest bronzes, it will do nobody any harm to consider the eight diagrams as the first attempt to express some sort of meaning by written signs. The eight diagrams were extended by king Wen to sixty-four, which were by him made the basis of the curious book called the Yi King, or Classic of Transformations.

The eight diagrams were supposed to be used to define the interaction of the elemental forces of nature and the effects of that interaction. The meanings attached to them by fortune-tellers in modern times are appended to the diagrams. The words immediately beneath them are their equivalent in Chinese.

THE EIGHT DIAGRAMS.

1. N.W., heaven, *yang*, celestial, producer, ether, humanity.
2. West, water, vapour ascending, fountains, pools, lightness.
3. South, fire, light, life, beauty, heat-giving, dynamic, warmth.
4. East, thunder, igneous exhalations, mover, stiffness.
5. S.E., wind, vapours, energy of expanse, flexibility.
6. North, water, liquid, elements, rigidity, cold.
7. N.E., mountains, solids, sustaining, motion, quiet, gravity.
8. S.W., earth, *yin*, terrestrial, recipient of corruption, drought.

Extract from *Williams' Dictionary*.

CHAPTER III.

SHANG DYNASTY.

With Modern Representative at left.

Kwei,
10th stem,
To consider,
representing Father
of Tang,
founder of Dynasty
(sole character on
vessel).

Tsu,
Grandfather,
ancestor.
Sin,
8th stem,
Acrid.

Hiung,
Elder brother.

Kwei,

Keng,
7th stem,
Metal
(sole character on
vessel).

Tsu,

Yi,

Fu,
Father,
Ting,
Adult man,
4th stem.

Fu,
Father,
Yi,
2nd stem,
Final particle,
Complete.

Fu,

Ren,
9th stem,
Great.

Fu Kwei.

Fu,

Fu Kia,
1st stem,
Bud, first.

Keng,

Fu,

Ren,
Man
(note its form).

Keng,

Kwei.

Tsu ting,

Hiung ting,

Fu sin,

Tsu,

Yi,

Mu,
Mother,

Sin,
Bitter,

Kwa,
Diagram.
(Evidence that
the diagrams
antedated Chow.)

Fu,

Chow,
Boat.

Yi,
Ting,

Tsu,
Kwei,

Mu,
Kwei,

Kwei,
Yi,

Son,

Grandson.

(This phrase continually used for " posterity.")

Tsu,

Swun,

Ko,
(Spear standing upright, Martial.)

Grandson,
(Figure upside down.)

Hing,
Walking,

Tsu,

Swun,

Chü,
To raise,

Che,
A cart,

Ping,
Grasp,
(A hand against sheaf.)

Chung,
Middle brother,

Chung,
Middle,

Mu,
Wood,

Chü,
To raise.

Tsu,

Swun,

Tsu,

Swun,

Ku,
Ancient.

Swun,
(Grandson holding
sword).

Yen,
Words, speech.

Tien,
A field.

Shi,
A generation
(3 tens).

Mu,
Mother.

Hu,
Tiger.

Ho,
Growing grain,
(2 stems, 1 figure.)

Grandson with bow.

Grandson holding
sword.

Fu,
Father.

Ting,
Tripod.

Ping,
Grasp.
(Hand holding sheaf
of grain.)

Chung,
Middle.

Unknown.

Ko,
Upright spear.

Grandson.

Grandson.

Mother.

Chow,
Boat.

Ro,
If.

Man, grasping
wood.

Kung,
Bow.

Yi,
Completed.

Chow,
Boat.

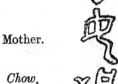

Che,
Cart.

Chow,
Boat.

Lung,
Dragon.

Shi,
A generation,
(3 tens.)

Grandson.

Two grandsons.

Tsu,

Ting,

Chow,
A besom.

Nü,
Woman.

K

Che,
To record.

You,
Friend,
(Two hands).

Chien,
To see.

Shi,
To serve.

Wu,
Negation.

Si,
Pewter.

Show,
Longevity.

Lai.
To rely on.

Pei,
Precious.

Hu,
Tiger.

Grandson.

Fu,
City.

Shi,
Arrow.

Grandson with
spear.

Ancestor.

(One of the 8 diagrams
incomplete on cover
of vessel.)

Show,
To receive.

One on body of vessel.
(See p. 140.)

Fu,
Hatchet.

Unknown.

Chung,
Middle brother.

Shi,
Generation,
(3 tens).

Footprints.

Tsu,
Foot.

Footprints,
Pronunciation
unknown.

Ting,
Adult man.

Er,
Ear.

Er,
Ear.

Chi,
Lance.

Tsu,
Foot.

Yue,
Battle axe.

Grandson.

Grandson.

Ear.

Foot.

Grandson.

Father.

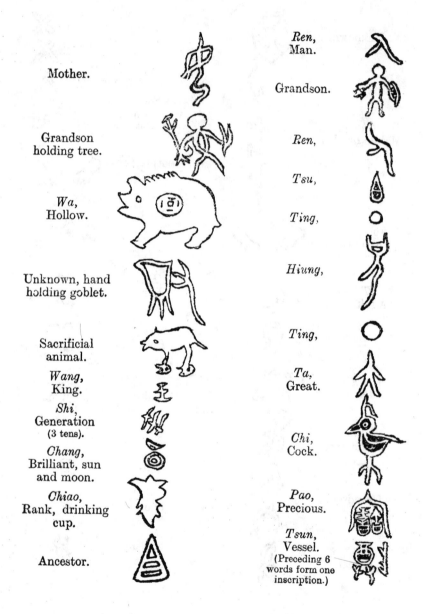

Mother.

Grandson
holding tree.

Wa,
Hollow.

Unknown, hand
holding goblet.

Sacrificial
animal.

Wang,
King.

Shi,
Generation
(3 tens).

Chang,
Brilliant, sun
and moon.

Chiao,
Rank, drinking
cup.

Ancestor.

Ren,
Man.

Grandson.

Ren,

Tsu,

Ting,

Hiung,

Ting,

Ta,
Great.

Chi,
Cock.

Pao,
Precious.

Tsun,
Vessel.
(Preceding 6
words form one
inscription.)

Ting, Sacrificial vessel.		*Keng,* 7th stem.
		Wu, Mid-day.
		Wang, King.
		Ming, Command.
		Chin, Sleep.
Fei, Negation.		*Miao,* Temple.
		Chen, Star.
		Chien, To see.
		Pei, North.
Ancestor.		*Tien,* Field.
		Szu, Four.
		Pin, Grade (3 mouths).
		Shi, Ten.
Son.		*Er,* Two.
		Yue, Moon.
Father.		*Tso,* To make.

Wan,
Myriad
(Scorpion form).

Chü,
To fear.

Ya,
(The square enclosure, signifying that the vessel was sanctified to temple use. Within it is the name *Chao fu.*)

Underneath is

Tsu,
Son.

Sin,
8th Stem.

Flag staff.

Chao,
Call.

Fu,
A man.

Tsu, Sin,

Yue,
Moon.

Unknown character.

Nai,
Also.

Moon,

Fish,

Foundation,

Complete
Inscription.

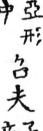

Complete in-
scription within
Ya:—

Chow, Boat.
Ting, Person.
Ro, If.
  Kwei, Son
holding flag.
Yi, *tsu*, Foot.
Yi, *fu*, City.

Ro,
If.

Son holding
standard.

Chü,
Fear.

Symbol
against
gluttony.

Chi,
A standard.

Grandson.

Unknown.

Unknown.

Hand
holding ear.

Chü,
Fear.

Same
in
Modern
Chinese.

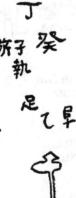

Ko,
Lance set up.

Chi,
Foundation.

Chung,
Middle.

CHAPTER IV.
CHOW, EARLY.

This inscription of seven characters was made on a sacrificial vessel to King Wen by his son Duke Chow, who was ruler of Lu, as Shantung was anciently styled. There are many examples of this inscription on numerous varieties of sacrificial bronzes. The style is in no respect dissimilar from that of the Shang dynasty.

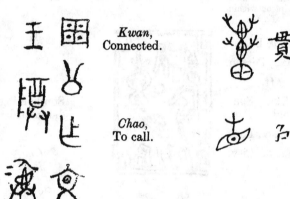

Kwan,
Connected.

Chao,
To call.

Siang,
Elephant.
(Figure from preceding dynasty.)

Above inscription in Modern Chinese.

Ru, or *Nai,*
Milk.

Chiw,
Nine.

Chien,
To see.

Hu,
Tiger.

Show,
The head.

Chen,
Minister.

Kwan,
Connected, strung together.

Tung (Sun in the trees), the East.	
Mu, Wood, tree.	
Chi, Banner.	
Tan, Solitary.	
Chiung, A lattice.	
Hu, Tiger.	
Siang, Looking among trees, mutually.	
Nan, South.	
Kwo, Kingdom.	
Shan, Mountain.	
Kwan, Connected.	

Wu, Negation. (Note two sides balancing = negation.)

Ma, Horse.

Unknown character.

Fu, City.

Two grandsons.

Ma, Horse (various).

Wu, Negation.

Liang, Bounds.

Unknown.

Min,
People.

Tsin,
Name of
Kingdom.

Pang,
Feudal State.

Yue,
Moon.

Chun,
Prince.

To,
Many

Fu, Happiness,
good luck.

Tsun, Honourable
(*vessel supported
by two hands*).

Ting,
Sacrificial vessel.

Chu,
A forest.

Siw,
Desist.

Tu, Earth.

Sheng,
Born, produced.
(Note growth out of
earth.)

Ho,
Grain.

Ho,
Grain.

Hing,
To walk,

Shi,
Business.

Numerals.

Shu,
Coarse grass cloth.

Two ancient forms of
Pei,
Precious.

Yuen,
Source.

Shan,
Mountain.

Hing,
To walk.

Kow,
Mouth.

Yue,
To speak.

Pu,
Negative.

Hien,
Manifest.

Hien,
Carriage roof.
Hia,
Below.
(When the shorter line
is above the meaning
is " above.")

CHAPTER V.

CHOW, LATER.

THE PO BELL OF CHOW.

The Chow dynasty seems to have been the first to introduce the bell as an instrument of music. The number of bells cast by the dynasty and its subordinate States was considerable. These are interesting for their design and workmanship, but especially for the inscriptions with which they were adorned in contemporary script. The bell, whose inscription is here reproduced, was called the Po, or large bell. It weighed 122½ catties (about 1¼ cwt.), and the inscription numbered 492 characters. They relate the institution of the State of Chi, in the north-west of Shantung. King Wu, in the early morning of a day in the fifth moon, ordered the Marquis of Kiang to march with his three armies of 3000 men to the eastern frontier of his newly established State of Chi to defend it against the wild men in the wilderness east of that frontier. His headquarters became the capital of the kingdom of Chi, and was situated where now stands the city of Lintzu hien, which was at once the eastern frontier of Chi and of the kingdom of Chow. The inscription records the ancient ancestry of the marquis and his marriage relationship. It states that he was cunning and brave as a tiger. The bell was cast by his admiring descendants and used at sacrificial honours to his memory. It is supposed that the bell was cast in the seventh century B.C., when Chi was prosperous. This was a century after the chaotic script had been reduced to order, and the one systematised set of characters introduced into general use. This inscription represents the script used by Confucius and after him up to the third century B.C., when Chin Shi Whang superseded it with a simpler, and when the square characters were devised which are still in use. The State of Chi was founded in 1122 B.C., and was absorbed by Chin in the third century B.C. Most of the ancient inscriptions on the vessels of the later Chow reproduced in the Po-ku-tu and the Siching kuchien are of the same style as that on the Po bell.

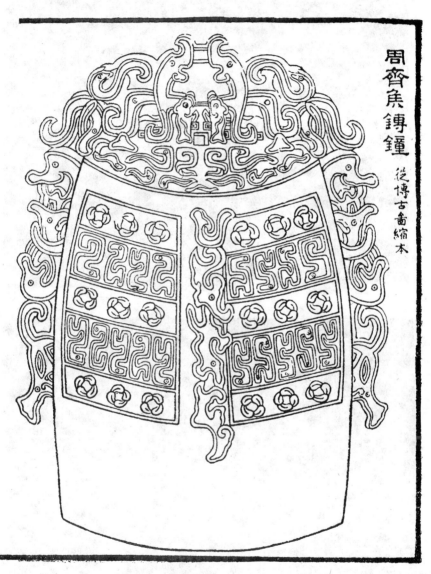

周齊戻鑄鐘 從博古畵縮本

THE PO BELL OF CHOW.

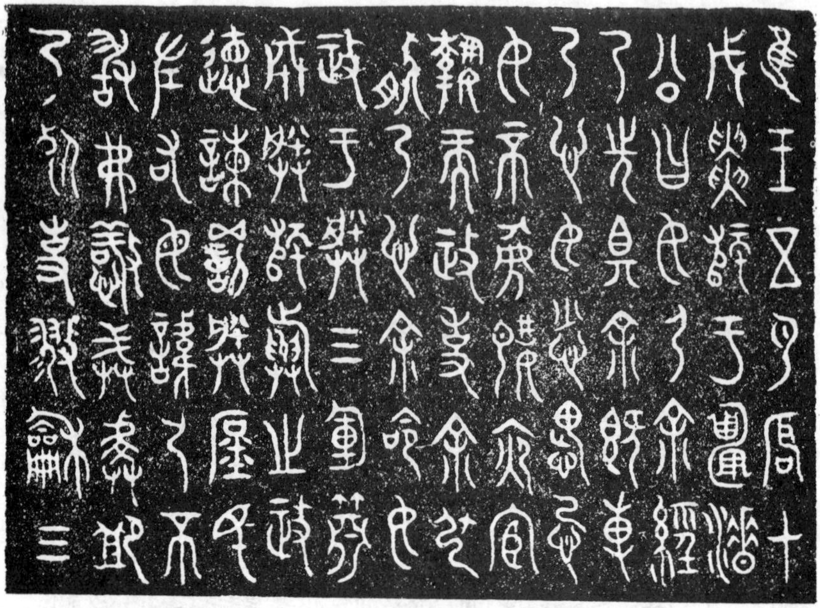

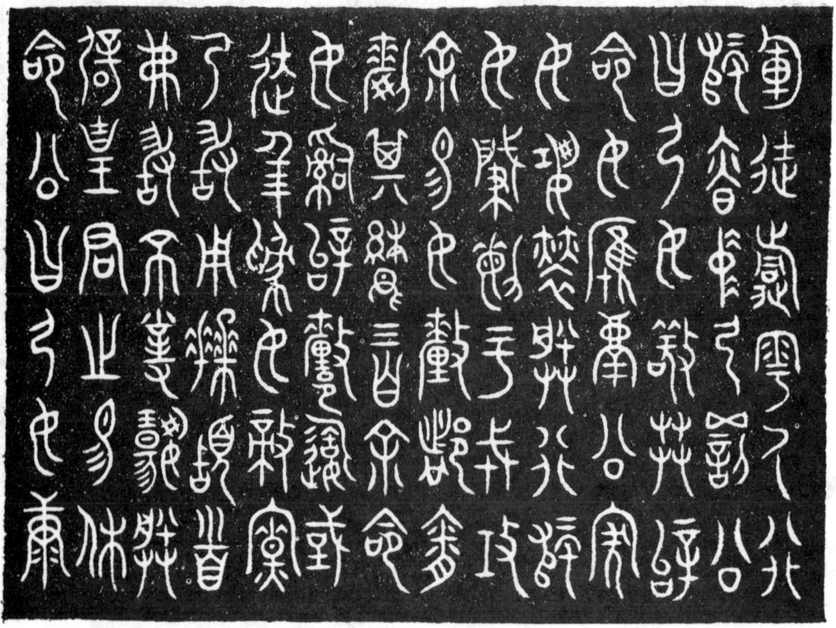

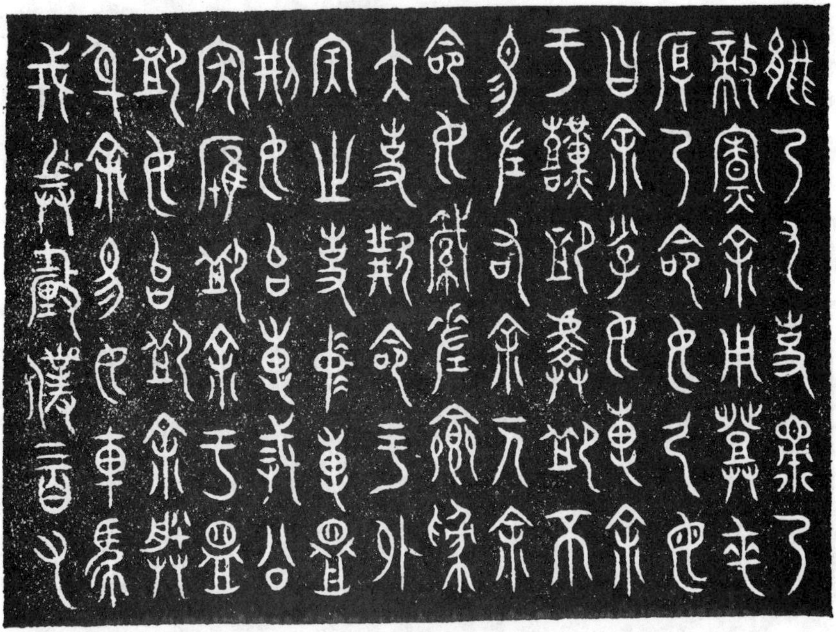

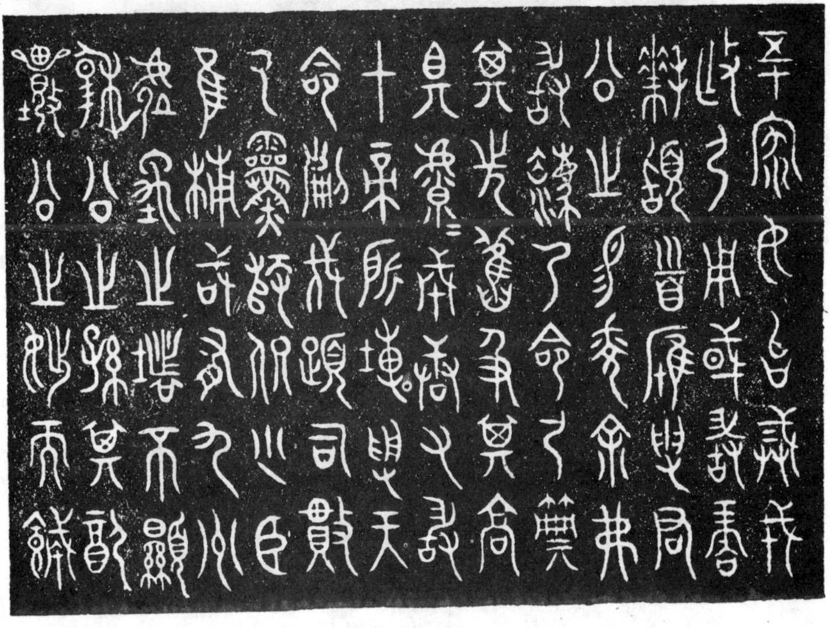

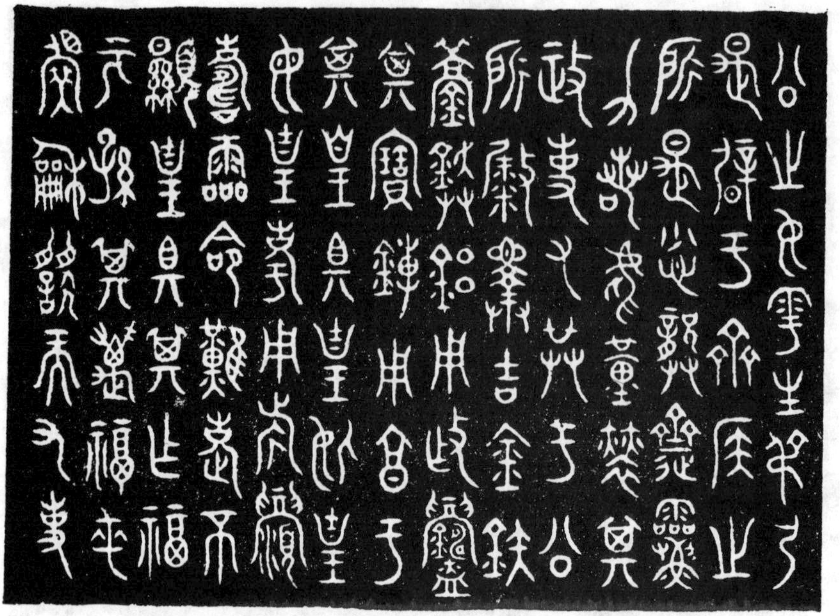

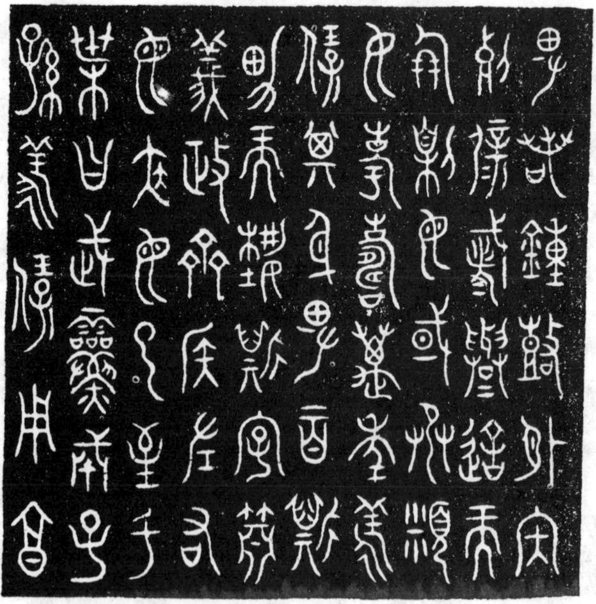

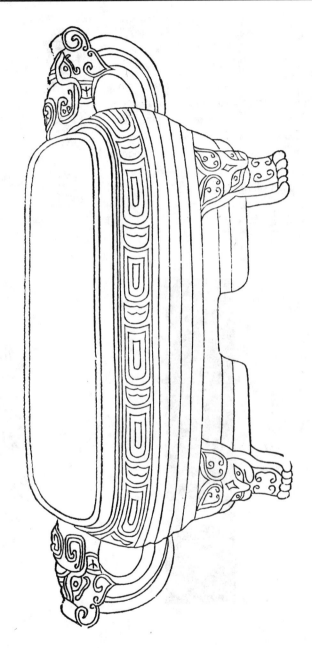

THE KUEI (Sacrificial Vessel).

KUEI.

The Kuei is a sacrificial vessel with rounded corners to represent heaven, which was believed to be circular. The title reads, *Chow How Kuei*, a *Kuei* in honour of How of Chow. The modern characters beside the inscription are a translation of the ancient.

CHOW

HOW

KUEI.

Ancient Chinese.

Modern Chinese.

鉴庚作旅籃

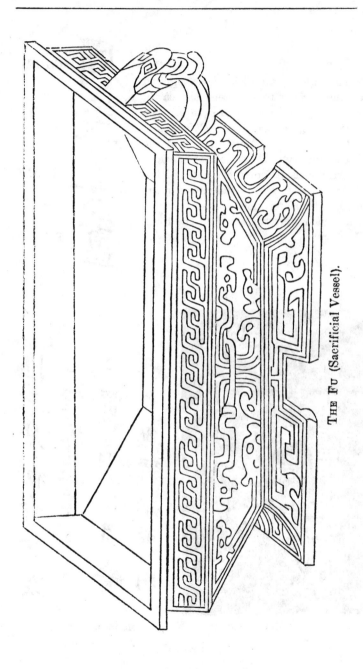

THE FU (Sacrificial Vessel).

FU.

The *fu* was a sacrificial vessel squared at the corners to represent the earth, which was supposed to be square. The title reads, *Chow Meng Chiang Fu*, a *fu* in honour of Meng Chiang of the Chow dynasty. The style of the ancient inscription is before the middle of the Chow dynasty. The small circles in the modern transliteration represent characters which were unknown to the Sung Scholars.

周 CHOW

孟 MENG

姜 CHIANG

簠 FU

惟正月初吉丁亥
〇侯作孟姜〇〇
〇簠用斷眉壽
〇無疆永壽用

Ancient Chinese.   **Modern Chinese.**

CHAPTER VI.

Chin.

A few specimens are given of the seal character of Chin to show that the small differences introduced are but slight modifications of the Chow characters. The fame of Chin as a literary reformer consists in the introduction of the square character.

集補泰山石刻全文

泰山石刻止存真點十字餘無可補闕全文
具載史記其縮刻于絳帖者猶存十之七
八今參以繹山琅邪諸以說文追摹斯
法集補四面全文以便觀摹

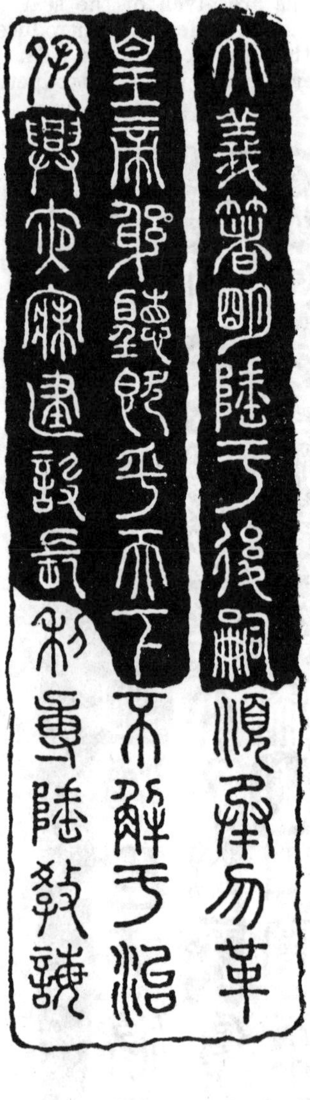

秦詛楚文

有秦嗣王敢用

吉王宣璧使其

宗祝邵鼜布憖
即王

告于不顯大神

巫咸及丕沈久
史記楚懷喜

湫以底楚之王熊
熊視此作熊相小異

相之多辠昔我

先君穆公及楚

成王是繆力同

心兩邦以壹絆

盟曰葉萬子孫

毋相為不利親

即不顯大神

咸大沈人湫而

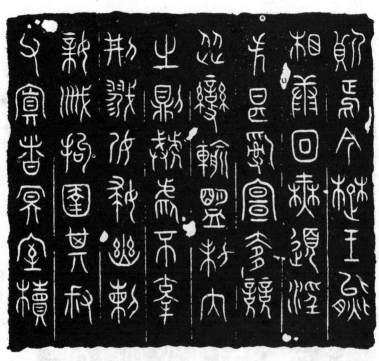

節馬今楚王熊

相爾回棘遐涇

芳邑雩宣參觀

沒麞輸盟製內
　即涌

光鼎棘為不辜
　　　　　朴婞

荊戮孚敘幽刺
　　　　　即毅

敦戚拘圍其林
　　　　　　即諸

父賓者賓室櫝

質鴈今楚王熊

相康回無道涇

侠甚乱宣參觀

従慶輸盟製内
　即涌

之卽麗麾不辜
　　　朴婞

刑戮孚敘幽刺
　　　　即毅

敦戚拘圍其林
　即諸

父賓者賓室櫝

秦嶧山碑　古刻久亡此從宋鄭文寶摹本　在西安府學

廿有六年，上薦高號，孝道顯明。既獻泰成，乃降專惠，親巡遠方。登于繹山，羣臣從者，咸思攸長。追念亂世，分土建邦……

CHAPTER VII.

HAN.

漢穀城長蕩陰令張遷碑 碑高九尺五寸廣三尺二寸計六行之四十二 字今在東平州學

篆額

漢故穀城長蕩陰令張君表頌

張君未沒乃云故者猶今言前任也前作穀城長後為蕩陰令漢制大縣曰令小縣曰長

君諱遷字公方陳留己吾
人也君之先出自有周周
宣王中興有張仲以孝友
為行披覽詩雅煥知其祖
高帝龍興有張良善用籌
策在帷幕之內決勝負千
里之外析珪於留文景之
間有張釋之建忠弼之謀
帝遊上林問禽狩所有苑
令不對更問嗇夫嗇夫事

漢魯相乙瑛請置孔廟百石卒史碑

碑高六尺　每行　字尚存　初元　又一寸　廣三又行

司徒臣雄司空臣戒稽首
言魯前相瑛書言詔書崇
聖道勉學藝孔子作春秋
制孝經刪述五經演易繫
辭經緯天地幽讚神明故
特立廟褒成侯四時來祠
事已即去廟有禮器無常
人掌領請置百石卒史一
人典主守廟春秋饗禮財
出王家錢給犬酒直須報

吳雄趙戒

學剛述三字尚存其邊洪民趺今補之

襃城庚孔均以西漢元始六年受封國在邲邱

犬酒謂犬与酒非犬酒

寵子孫敬恭卹礼傳于曰
用衆〇長吏備〇〇歆知
〇〇漢制作先世所歆尊祠
如瑛言孔子大聖則象乾
大司農給米祠臣愚以為
尹給爵羊豕雞〇〇各一
皆備大宰大常祝臨祠河南
子孫大大常祝令各孔人
行祠先聖師侍祠者孔子
郭玄霹對故事辟雍禮未
謹問太常祠曹掾馮〇史

制

極可許臣請魯相爲孔子
廟置百石卒史一人掌領
禮器出王家錢給一大酒直
他如故事臣雄臣頓首死罷
誠惶誠恐頓首頓首死罷
死罷臣稽首以聞
日可
元嘉三年三月廿七日壬
寅奏雒陽宮
字季高河南原武吳雄

漢開母廟石闕銘

黃帝初祖　德币于虞　虞帝始祖　德币子新　歲在大梁　龍集戊辰　戊辰直定　天命有民　據土德受

黃帝初祖　德币于虞　虞帝始祖　德币子新　歲在大梁　龍集戊辰　戊辰直定　天命有民　據土德受

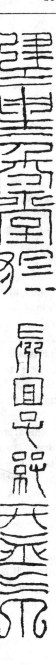

Han Dynasty, in the beginning of the Christian era introduced this style of seal character, which is a complete change from preceding styles: it is square and symmetrical. Since its introduction it has been the favourite style for all stamps and seals.

CHAPTER VIII.

Tablet of Yu.

These remarkable characters are copied from an inscription engraved on a stone tablet set up on the famous mountain Heng Shan in Hunan. It purports to have been cut by Yu, who reigned in the beginning of the twenty-third century B.C. Though in the original inscription the " flood which overspread the land " is referred to, there is nothing in the text which claims to be the work of Yu's hands. The four small characters at the end ascribing it to Yu are by a different hand in a modern style. The tablet has disappeared. The inscription itself affords no clue to the time of cutting. The script gives ample evidence that it was not cut within two thousand years of Yu The characters are of a uniform style suggesting birds' heads craning to make up the words. They are symmetrically balanced in a fashion unknown to the ancients before the time of Chin Shi whang, and fully developed only in the time of the Han dynasty. There are some grotesque specimens of the time of Chin Shi whang, which, though suggestive of kinship, are neither so uniform nor in so free a style as is this entire inscription. In the earlier dynasties, though there are variations of form, there is nothing approaching these forms. A few of the tablets of Chin may have suggested to a clever scholar the idea of cutting out such an inscription. Previous to that time there is nothing in the least approaching it. Here there is variety of form in uniformity of style. The inscription is presented as a curiosity and a clever forgery—if, indeed, it is supposed to represent the ancient form of character. Judging from the styles of the ancient past, this inscription was made by no one previous to the Christian era.

右常禹刊

碑末四楷書
後人所增

奉   寔竄辟永   儵萬國其   亨衣制食   從南潰狩

CHAPTER IX.

MAN.

To illustrate the ingenuity of the Chinese scholars in composing new words and the elasticity of the language in making new combinations, a few selections follow borrowed from the dictionary Shuo wen. The selections are the simplest of the long list of words under the heading "man." Though few, they suffice to show the genius of the language for self-propagation and extension, and its unique sphere among languages.

The first two words are the ancient and modern forms of the word for "man." Though ancient, the first word is by no means the most ancient, specimens of which are seen under the phrases and words of the Shang list, which are the most ancient known. The form in the Shuo wen is of the Han style, fifteen or more centuries after the Shang. It is well to compare the form with the character "man" under the list of the Shang dynasty (p. 141).

Man, ancient and modern form.

Man and son, to nourish.

Man with two, signifies relatives.

Two men with a line out from one, sig. arms outstretched.

Man with scholar, to learn.

Man with white, signifies older.

Man with middle, sig. middle brother.

Man with two fires, signifies comfort.

Man with two scholars, sig. good.

Man with demon, sig. admirable.
(Demon as in Greek, spirit of departed.)

Man with mouth and scholar, sig. correct.

Two men, means resemblance.

Man with two men under cover, to lean on.

Man with "but," because.

Man with ear, secondary.

Man with a vessel, perpendicular, or to stand erect.

Man with five, squad of five.

Man with ten, squad of ten.

Man with 100, squad of hundred.

Man with agreement, harmony.

Man with completed, image.

Man with happiness, rejoice.

Two men back to back,
enemy.

Man on a hill,
hillman, high.

Man upside down,
change.

Man with another
upside down,
teacher.

Man with his back
turned, to meet one

Man and high,
sight-seeing.

Two men facing same
direction,
mutually hearing.

Two men both with
back turned,
secret.

Two men back to back,
violent.

Two men above the level,
difficult, high.

Three men,
multitude.

Man with child,
humble.

Man with official,
small official.

Man with a field,
boy.

Man and only,
lazy.

Man with open
mouth and sun,
sing for joy.

Man with foot
behind,
persecute.

Man with three
fields, defeated and
scattered.

Man, and two with
backs to him,
parting, separate.

Man with three
scholars and man
below a line,
pigmy.

Man with long life,
to heal.

Man with open
mouth accusing two
first of falsehood,
to doubt.